Art, Sex, Politics

By William Eaton

Art, Sex, Politics

By William Eaton

Serving House Books

Art, Sex, Politics

Copyright © 2017 William Eaton Warner

All drawings are also copyright © 2017 William Eaton Warner

All rights reserved.

No part of this book may be used or reproduced in any manner whatsoever without the prior written permission of the copyright holder except for brief quotations in critical articles or reviews.

ISBN: 978-0-9977797-8-3

Cover design by Molly Renda

Interior design and layout by Walter Cummins
Serving House Books logo by Barry Lereng Wilmont

Published by Serving House Books
Copenhagen, Denmark, Florham Park, NJ
SERVING HOUSE BOOKS WEST, LLC
8119 Defiance Ave. Las Vegas, NV 89129

www.servinghousebooks.com

Member of The Independent Book Publishers Association

First Serving House Books Edition 2017

Contents

Great Teachers & Humble Drawings — 7

It would be nice to set out without any baggage

[1] DON'T HATE ME HATE — 11

[2] Drawing, Conversation, Life — 14

[3] Guston Presidents Cartoons Questions? — 16
  Afterword on Nixon, Kennedy, Trump, Clinton, the UN, the World Series—Our Values?

[4] My Evening with Marta — 25

[5] On Savoring — 33

Art

[6] The Third Man — 55

[7] Dickinson's Dying Tiger — 60

[8] Guston, Schapiro, Rosenberg, . . . Dialogue — 70

[9] Collage, TV President, Bonnard, Miró — 89

Sex

[10] Carol, Rooney! Smoking? Gun — 99

[11] On Shunga and Learning How to Feel What When — 105

[12] Distancing / Awareness — 110

[13] Professional Primates — 121

Politics

[14] The American Flag is at Half-Mast Today — 129

[15] Ditch the Term Pathogen — 134

[16] NRALGBTQ — 141

[17] In Kant's Wood — 146

    Afterword—Of making much of trees there is no end

[18] The Beauty of the System — 164

Closing Words

[19] Sonnet for 9/27 — 171

[20] Bologna Postmodernism Bob Perelman Amis — 173

[21] Friendship, Deception, Writing — 179

[22] Sontag, Hell, Thinking, Politics — 197

[23] Almost Pure Pleasures — 209

    Afterword—Social Comments

Backmatter

Where have we been? — 215

Thanks! — 219

Ways of Skipping Around — 221

About the Author — 225

Great Teachers & Humble Drawings

This book is dedicated to several great teachers who have helped me take my ideas and my reading further than they could ever have gone without them. I have in mind five professors, four of them Americans: Steven Affeldt, who gave me a rich way of reading Wittgenstein; the late Robert Blauner, who introduced me to the possibilities of sociology; Gerald Press, who gave me a rich way of reading Plato, and Mitchell Miller, who, though a Plato scholar, in his youth introduced me to Marx.

Drafting the "In Kant's Wood" essay while in France brought back memories from long ago—briefly studying philosophy, at l'Université Paris 8, with Jean-François Lyotard, best known for his writing on postmodernism. As I recall, before turning to Lucretius's *clinamen* (the possibility of change), we spent several classes on just one or two paragraphs of one of Kant's Critiques. Thus I was introduced to the French method of *explication de texte*, which has but faint equivalents in the principal approaches to philosophical study pursued in the United States. Professor Lyotard also introduced me to a fundamental, disturbing truth that Americans continue to have great difficulty appreciating: in the twentieth century—what with two world wars, the Holocaust, Hiroshima, and the rise of environmental concerns—the Enlightenment project, however seductive it may remain, reached its gruesome end. Henry Adams might say that my education began there.

THE DRAWINGS were inspired by a practice of Cy Twombly's: drawing in the dark, unable to see either what one is drawing or how one is drawing it. Twombly apparently used this technique, in his youth, to get away from figurative drawing. For me it has become a way to give the unconscious a larger role, to escape from "the right" (conventional standards, the super-ego), and to simplify, in the sense of reducing the number of lines.

Notes

"Distancing / Awareness" was originally a talk at a 2014 Association of Graduate Liberal Studies Programs (AGLSP) conference, the theme of which was "Revolutions: Past, Present, and Future." The text has been substantially revised for publication here. "In Kant's Wood" was presented at the Michigan Academy's 2015 conference.

Earlier versions of the following have been previously published—
- *"The Beauty of the System" (*sans *introduction) in* Choices: A Chapbook *(World Voices, Web del Sol).*
- *"Friendship, Deception, Writing: Within and Beyond Plato's Lysis" in* Agni *in 2016.*
- *"Bologna Postmodernism Bob Perelman Amis"—with pictures and captions and a postmoderny layout—by the* Literary Explorer *in 2015. Can be found on-line.*

Versions of the other texts first appeared either in Zeteo *(Zeteojournal.com) or* Montaigbakhtinian *(Montaigbakhtinian.com).*

Publishers are thanked for allowing these pieces to reappear in the present collection. Most all the texts published here are available, in some form, on-line, and the on-line versions may include notes, links, and references not included here.

[I]
It would be nice to set out without any baggage

One of the greatest blessings that the United States could receive in the near future would be to have her industries halted, her business discontinued, her people speechless, a great pause in the world of affairs created. . . . We should be hushed and silent, and we should have the opportunity to learn what other people think.

> — John Cage, "Other People Think," speech delivered at the Hollywood Bowl, 1928

[1]
DON'T HATE ME HATE

A PRE-TRUMP ART EXHIBIT OR SPECTACLE at Paris's official hip museum, *le Palais de Tokyo*, offered, among many other things, incomplete slogans, handwritten with black markers on cardboard. Among the dozens of these, most of which were in French, I noted and translated these:

WE ARE THE FORGOTTEN OF

NO DEMOCRACY WITHOUT

I DON'T WANT A FUTURE I WANT A

SHARING WILL SAVE THE

A ROOF IS A

LET'S SHARE THE WEALTH INSTEAD OF

PEACE AND

The exhibit, *Flamme éternelle*, was produced by a Swiss artist, Thomas Hirschorn, and contained a lot more—Styrofoam blocks and bits, couches and arm chairs wrapped in packing tape, graffiti, piles of tires, a bar, books, computers, and TVs and DVDs for watching Hollywood movies, people talking and reading into microphones, words projected by loudspeakers, simulated ghetto "fires" (or were these Olympic torches?) around which people were supposed to sit, . . .

There was plenty to dislike, but I was immediately charmed by the incompleteness of the slogans. I had a sinking feeling that Hirschorn's idea was that he was empowering each of us to complete the slogans in our own way, but . . . Sometimes the subconscious wins out over the meager products of our conscious minds?

Intentionally or not, the incomplete slogans called attention to the fact that, at that moment in history—but perhaps no longer, not since the 2016 US election?—we did not know how to write complete slogans, we did not know what to stand for. Was this a warning sign or an oasis in a vast desert? On the negative side, there is the fact that advertising and corporations are so rife with slogans, and our incapacity may also have been connected to a lack of solidarity. Slogans assume that large groups of people can and should unite around simple ideas. And perhaps we weren't lacking for simplicity, but for a sense that there was much of interest—or much of anyone or anything?—beyond the borders of "me." (Some readers might take this—as well as the title of this brief piece—to apply to Donald Trump in particular.)

ON THE OTHER SIDE of *le Palais*'s vast and cacophonous basement spaces, as part of Monte Laster's *Banlieue is Beautiful* show/spectacle/happening, I found, in one corner of the cement floor, the sorts of complete statements that individuals still could and indeed still do make. Words to live by, should we call these?

These statements were included in colorful small paintings that offered the footprints, names, and favorite colors and sayings of several citizens of La Courneuve, a not-wealthy suburb (*banlieue*) or series of housing projects north-east of Paris. La Courneuve, which was the scene of violent riots a few years ago, is where both Laster (native of Texas) and Mébrouka Hadjadj, the painter, were living and making their art. Among the statements (not slogans) that Hadjadj's paintings presented were:

> From Matilda Mijajlovic, a 55-year-old woman looking for a paying job: "J'ai décidé d'être heureuse parce que c'est bon pour la santé." I decided to be happy because it's good for your health.

> From Laila El Moueddine, simply self-described as a citizen—"citoyenne." This word may recall the French Revolution and a slogan that had its origins then: Liberté, Egalité, Fraternité. Freedom, Equality, Solidarity. Laila El Moueddine's statement: "Perdre tout espoir, c'est la liberté." To lose all hope, that's liberty.

"Freedom's just another word for nothin' left to lose" is how

American pop culture has memorialized this. Or, if you really want to know freedom, wait until you've lost everything.

Now, in the wake of the 2016 US Presidential election, many Leftish people, and people in the art world, and not just in the United States, feel that there remains a great deal to be lost, or to be fought for, some last full measure of freedom included. It is also the case that at such moments—of civil war, basically—there is a tendency to complete slogans hastily and to imagine that life is simpler than it is.

The incomplete "hate" slogan at *le Palais de Tokyo* was not exactly as I have recorded it here, but "DON'T HATE ME HATE MY"?

[2]

Drawing, Conversation, Life

MOST ARTISTS, BEFORE THEY HAVE BEGUN TO DRAW—in a studio, with a model—have made any number of decisions. What materials they are going to work with and on; the scale of the work; what sort of results they hope to achieve—a likeness? classically proportioned beauty? an evocative gesture? This outline allows us to speak of another, ideal drawing process in which decisions would not have been made. Perhaps the artist ends up doing nothing, or at least not making any marks, and this without shame. The artist's hand and eye respond to the model, the moment, the lighting, her own emotions and emotions in the room, her technical capacities and limitations, political and economic circumstances surrounding the room, . . . All of which might paralyze or inspire the artist, but could, more likely, less extremely, result in art works that, however great or small, are of their time and place.

This outline allows us to speak of an ideal conversation which would begin, or not begin, amid similar aspirations. Two people—strangers or friends—find themselves intersecting, perhaps seated facing one another, sharing a meal, perhaps side by side in an elevator or walking out of an abs-butt-and-thighs class together. Of course often (always?) there are things we need to say to someone, anyone, to another human being. But in the particular ideal process I am sketching here, any such need is no more than faint. Above all there is this other person who is sharing space with us and who is, to at least some degree, open to hearing what we may say. "I" respond to "you" and you to me, and there is—like a boat blown by a wind across some surface of a vast sea—a conversation.

Might we then go on to speak of an ideal way to live—without planning, but with our eyes, ears, and hearts open, with our hands and our lips ready to respond to others, to our circumstances and feelings? We might.

Although, of course, the artist through drawing learns things, or his hands and eyes do. And if we talk with someone a second, third, fourth time, our minds are no longer unfilled. We come to these subsequent conversations laden, at times happily, with material that cannot be unchosen.

[3]
Guston Presidents Cartoons Questions?

IN A NUMBER OF PHILIP GUSTON'S more than 100 cartoon-style drawings of Richard Nixon, which were made in sketchbooks in 1971 and 1975, the former President's nose and jowls are transformed into a cock and balls (or scrotum). We recognize the long-standing association of the nose and the penis, and can understand that Guston, in his sixties, was making his way back from Abstract Expressionism toward the cartooning of his adolescence. He was exaggerating the features of Nixon's face that begged to be exaggerated, that many cartoonists during that period were exaggerating. He was making vulgar—much as a boy, or girl, in a midnight subway station draws a cock and balls on an advertising poster. But why the repetitiveness? What might have been working its way through the mature artist's mind as he sketched variations on this same idea—President Nixon's face as a cock and balls, and "bone/boner" jokes—again and again?

Well, not to add further vulgarity, but there was the idea in the late Sixties and early Seventies that Nixon was fucking America. Guston makes this point most explicit in his 1971 drawing of a cock-nose pushing into a bare ass labelled U.S.A. This is in line with slogans of those times such as "Nixon pull out [of the Vietnam War] like your father should have" and "Dick Nixon before he dicks you."

The drawings were hardly seen until 2001, more than twenty years after Guston's death. In 2001 The University of Chicago Press reproduced 73 of the works in *Philip Guston's Poor Richard*. In 2016, in the run-up to the Trump-Clinton election, the Hauser & Wirth art gallery in New York featured these drawings again. Visiting the gallery's interior, white-walled rooms, one could get a strong sense of the impotence felt by the artist—or, if you prefer, of the impotence of artists. The President and his cronies were screwing the country, and all an artist could do was draw over and over again the President's cock-nose.

"Draw your own cock!" one might exclaim. An old friend, Carol Wills, now in her seventies, recently sent me a poem she'd written about her breasts:

> These breasts
>
> need to *breathe*, to *float*,
>
> to roll from one side to the other.

There's a certain self-assurance and glee in those lines (from a longer poem), and in writing a poem about your breasts, or even your elbows. Carol proposed that I write a poem about my testicles. I replied that I was more inclined to try to follow in E.E. Cummings wake—"i like my body when it is with your / body." But to draw another man's, a more powerful man's, cock-nose over and over again?

COMING AT OUR SUBJECT FROM ANOTHER ANGLE, and with help from French literature, we may note that, right from the start, there is sadness is in Edmond Rostand's wonderful, big-nose-centered romantic comedy, *Cyrano de Bergerac*. From Act I, Scene i:

> Un nez ! . . . Ah ! messeigneurs, quel nez que ce nez-là ! . . .
>
> On ne peut voir passer un pareil nasigère
>
> Sans s'écrier : « Oh ! non, vraiment, il exagère ! »
>
> Puis on sourit, on dit : « Il va l'enlever . . . »
>
> Mais Monsieur de Bergerac ne l'enlève jamais.
>
> A nose!—ah, my lords, what a nose that is! You can't
> see such a noseliness go by without crying aloud:
> "Oh, no! it goes too far! And then, with a smile,
> one says, "He's going to take it off." But that nose
> Monsieur de Bergerac never takes off.

Philip Guston (né Goldstein) and Richard Nixon were both

born in 1913 and both grew up in Southern California; Guston a Jew, Nixon a Quaker. Nicely, I might describe myself as half Jewish, half Quaker. Many would say I have a "Jewish nose," and this even as many would say that I am a clone of my father, of the WASP line of the family. A Jew may come to feel sensitive about his or her nose, and not least because of all the cartoons, jovial and vicious, that have been drawn of Jews, making much of their/our noses. An American Medical Association journal article from 2001 states that "some plastic surgery texts continue to describe the 'Jewish nose' as if it were a standard physical deformity requiring surgical correction." This says less about noses than about how the medical profession seeks to drum up business. However, there is certainly a long, prominent, and often-mocked tradition of Jewish girls from upwardly mobile American families getting nose jobs, and in the Nixon era the result was often described as a "ski-jump" nose. Richard Nixon had a very pronounced ski-jump nose, though presumably not as a result of surgery.

A next question then: What could be the significance of a Jew drawing a WASP's big nose over and over again? « Oh ! non, Monsieur Guston, vraiment, il exagère ! » But no, it may not be possible for a Jewish artist to go too far in this case. As if to say, OK, we're deformed, we're grotesque, but so are you.

I recall one weekend night of my youth, around the same time that Guston was doing his first Nixon drawings. Some of us were on acid, some just having fun, wandering around our university town, and whenever someone made an assertion, one of our company, a beautiful girl, Jewish, who I was much taken with, would agree with the assertion and say, to the group as a whole, "That's why we're friends." As if these were things of which constant reminder was needed—that we agreed, that we were friends. And thus I can imagine—while Philip drew compulsively late at night in his rural studio, nose after nose—his unconscious saying over and over, as if to Richard, "This is why we're friends."

The Hauser & Wirth press release on the show states: "Guston's distress over the political situation was fueled by conversations with his friend, the writer Philip Roth. The artist and the writer shared an intellectual disposition for the mundane 'crapola' of American popular culture." This leads us back to Roth's 1958-59 novella *Goodbye Columbus*, in which the main female character, Brenda Patimkin, a New Jersey suburban "Jewish American Princess," as such people used to be called, has had a nose job. Roth describes the objection of the male protagonist, Neil Klugman, who lives with his aunt and uncle in Newark and works at the public library. Brenda's old nose fitted her father well, Neil observes. "There was a bump in it, all right; up at the bridge it seemed as though a small eight-sided diamond had been squeezed in under the skin. . . . I knew Mr. Patimkin would never bother to have that stone cut from his face, and yet, with joy and pride, no doubt, had paid to have Brenda's diamond removed and dropped down some toilet in Fifth Avenue Hospital."

I find on-line this explication from "College Essay Help":

> Why is this such a big deal to Neil? Well, the story is set post-World War II. The Holocaust was a very recent memory for many Jewish people. Neil might think that by altering her nose, a physical testament to her Jewish heritage, she is bowing to people who discriminate against Jews and hurting herself in the process. Sadly, he hurts her too by not accepting her current physical state and passing judgment on Brenda and her family.

THERE ARE MANY REPETITIONS in Guston's series of drawings. These include the Klan-like hoods which also appear in Guston paintings from this period. Also repeated: "Key Biscayne," which is where Nixon held property and had close friends, both of which—the property and the friends—became connected with the sort of scandals, court cases, etc., in which both Donald Trump and the Clintons have been entangled. Another set of words that reoccurs in Guston's work, "It seems like an impossible dream." This is a line from the most famous passage from one of Nixon's most famous (and televised, widely heard) speeches, addressing the Republican National Convention in Miami Beach, accepting the Republican presidential nomination, in 1968. The passage begins:

> I see another child tonight. He hears the train go by at night and he dreams of faraway places where he'd like to go. It seems like an impossible dream. But he is helped on his journey through life. A father who had to go to work before he finished the sixth grade, sacrificed everything he had so that his sons could go to college. A gentle, Quaker mother, with a passionate concern for peace, quietly wept when he went to war but she understood why he had to go.

As a "birthright Quaker," Nixon could have gotten an exemption from the draft and military service—and Quakers would say that he should have! But this would, inter alia, have been un-American, have put him ever on the fringe of American life. Nixon, 28 when the United States declared war on Japan, opted to enlist in the Navy and ended up doing things like supervising the loading and unloading of cargo aircraft at Guadalcanal.

Nixon's convention speech went on:

> A great teacher, a remarkable football coach, an inspirational minister encouraged him on his way. A courageous wife and loyal children stood by him in victory and also defeat.
>
> And in his chosen profession of politics, first there were scores, then hundreds, then thousands, and finally millions worked for his success. And tonight he stands before you—nominated for President of the United States of America.
>
> You can see why I believe so deeply in the American Dream.

An impossible dream, yes, although more typically, people on the Left, people like my parents, would have used a word like "nightmare." Along with Senator Joseph McCarthy himself, Richard Nixon was the Republican most associated with what has come to be called McCarthyism: the practice of seeking to increase or consolidate one's own power and that of one's allies by accusing other people of disloyalty, subversion, or treason. During the Mc-

Carthy period, the accused were often Jews and always they were people on the Left, people who were often known as advocates for social justice, for working people, and so forth. As I have written elsewhere, those who made use of proto-McCarthyite tactics included people like Walt Disney, whose great interest was in preventing his illustrators and other staff from defending and advancing their own interests (e.g. in becoming better paid). And before McCarthy's rise to prominence, the Mafia played a large role in developing and carrying out the war on wage laborers.

An Authentic History Center post on McCarthyism notes that Nixon's political career began in 1946 when he ran for Congress against an incumbent Democrat, Jerry Voorhis, a loyal supporter of the New Deal with a liberal voting record. Nixon suggested that Voorhis's endorsement by a group linked to communists meant that Voorhis must have radical left-wing views. In reality, Voorhis was a staunch anti-communist. He had once been voted by the press corps as the "most honest congressman." But Nixon was able to successfully link Voorhis to the group linked to the communists, and Nixon's political career was launched.

When we ask why the line—"It seems like an impossible dream"—had meaning for Guston, we may note his father—a Jew in a Southern California that at the beginning of the twentieth century was riddled with anti-Semitism, with the local Ku Klux Klan leading the anti-Semitic charge—Louis Goldstein had been unable to find decent work. A blacksmith, for a while he scratched out a living as a junk collector, and then hung himself. Philip, about 10 years old at the time, was the first to find his father's body. As a Los Angeles adolescent, as much later in his Woodstock studio, he found refuge in drawing cartoons.

Afterword on Nixon, Kennedy, Trump, Clinton, the UN, the World Series—Our Values?

It is important to keep in mind that on the Democratic side, McCarthy's biggest supporters were the Kennedys, and, unfortunately,

Trump and his allies may now, in reviving McCarthyist tactics, be adding a new chapter to this story. In his youth Trump's mentor was Roy Cohn, who became famous for his aggressive questioning of suspected communists when he was the Chief Counsel on the US Senate's Permanent Subcommittee on Investigations during the "McCarthy hearings," 1953-54. It is said that Cohn, who was from a Jewish family, beat out Robert Kennedy for the McCarthy committee job in part to help the committee avoid accusations of an anti-Semitic bias.

From Arthur Herman (an historian who has been a fellow at the conservative Hudson Institute), *Joseph McCarthy: Reexamining the Life and Legacy of America's Most Hated Senator*:

> John Kennedy's views, on communism and the Soviet threat, were not so different from McCarthy's . . . One night in February 1952 he heard a speaker at Harvard's Spree Club denounce McCarthy in the same breath as Alger Hiss [a New Deal liberal who played a large role in the founding of the United Nations and then was accused, before the House Un-American Activities Committee, of being a Soviet spy]. Kennedy shot back, "How dare you couple the name of a great American patriot [i.e. McCarthy] with that of a traitor [i.e. Hiss]!"

It might have been thought that Kennedy's and Nixon's support for McCarthyism, a movement and approach notable for its lack of integrity, would have led to their disgrace, would have made them unelectable once McCarthyism began to be widely and prominently denounced. But no, both of these people were then elected to be Presidents of the United States.

And thus I was not surprised, yet still more than dismayed to read one of the facts—or no, all of the facts!—reported in Jonathan M. Katz's September 2016 *New York Times* story "U.N. Admits Role in Cholera Epidemic in Haiti." The epidemic, Katz reminded readers, had "killed at least 10,000 people and sickened hundreds of thousands." The United Nations had finally, in 2016, acknowledged that its "stabilization mission" in Haiti (a.k.a. MINUSTAH) played a role in the disaster, because some of the peacekeepers who came to serve in Haiti had brought the cholera virus with them and because the mission was still discharging its waste into public canals *even four years after the epidemic began*. And so—we come to the additional dismaying fact—what was the fate of Edmond Mulet, the Guatemalan diplomat who was the head of MINUSTAH when the epidemic began? Was he, say, fired? Demoted? No, the UN promoted him—to be Chief of Staff to Secretary-General Ban Ki-moon.

Was it his long involvement in Latin American politics, peace negotiations, and relations with the United States that got Mulet promoted, or a reputation for incompetence? Was it that he had proved good at something that the previous Secretary-General, Kofi Annan, had also, on his way up the ladder, proved good at? Had Mulet proved that, in the midst or on the verge of humanitarian disaster, he was capable of doing nothing, of accepting his or his organization's impotence, of not speaking out loudly in an attempt to prevent the deaths of thousands?

The more general question here is: What do such phenomena tell us about our society and its values and about those who we would put in key figurehead (if not real leadership) positions? The following may seem trivial when compared to McCarthyism or to the killing of 10,000 innocent people, but, on the day I went to the Nixon drawings show at Hauser & Wirth, I happened to tune in the Fox broadcast of the baseball World Series. Before the game, announcers and former baseball stars were shown behind a podium, and they gave their opinions on which team was likely to win and so forth. One of the questions that before the 2016 election was often asked about Trump and Clinton was: in a country with 300 million people, are these two people really the best two presidential candidates we can come up with? So, who were the two former baseball stars Fox came up with to put on national television? Alex Rodriquez, one of the most prominent users of banned performance-enhancing drugs, and Pete Rose, who agreed to permanent ineligibility from baseball amid accusations that he gambled on baseball games while playing for and managing a major league team. Lack of integrity comes to seem a prerequisite for gaining prominent positions in our society.

Could this be, say, because the truly powerful in the society know they can count on the corrupt, spineless, or ductile to be corruptible, spineless, or ductile as and when necessary? Or could it be that prominent corruptness, spinelessness, or ductility—or incompetence—provides a kind of blanket excuse for all the rest of our misdeeds? Or . . . ?

[4]
My Evening with Marta
A few notes on sexuality in the workplace

HOW MANY HOURS OF MY LIFE have I spent in offices? Roughly 2,000 a year times more than 30 rough years. That's not only a lot of empty or trivial hours, but also a lot of collegial relationships with women to whom I have been sexually attracted. And at times it has seemed that these women have been attracted to me, too. And there are also women who seem attracted to me although I am not attracted to them, and women to whom I am attracted, but who seem to have no interest in me. And there are parallel worlds, or corridors, in which my gay and lesbian colleagues are enjoying, wrestling with, and ignoring their erotic feelings.

In recent months I have at times found myself discussing various technical matters with one "Marta," and during these discussions there has been an excitement in her eyes and her voice, an openness to her posture (to her legs), that have seemed to have little to do with the enervatingly dry and disconnected subjects that we are paid to discuss. (Or you might say that we are involved in a complex charade; we are paid to unwittingly disguise the neo-colonial objectives of our organization, and one of the ways we do this is by taking seriously matters that are not really serious at all.)

Marta seems to be developing a habit of coming by my office when her work day is done, exchanging a few light-hearted, not work-related words before she goes home to her husband, who is in some way debilitated, and to her son, now old enough to look out for himself. I appreciate Marta's visits, and I should also say that, while I have considered the possibility that she and I might have an affair, this has not seemed like something I want to do. And, as far as I know, Marta, consciously or unconsciously, agrees with me. There are aspects of me and my company that she likes, and I can well imagine she likes the fact that my eyes, voice, and posture reveal that I find her attractive and engaging. She may well like the fact that I, a senior colleague, have complimented her on aspects of her work, but affair may well not be on her list.

So why I am dragging readers through all this? Well, for one, my sense is that I am describing a not-untypical work relationship; many of us these days have these kinds of relationships. Secondly—and this is what led me to begin work on this piece—the other evening when Marta came to my office and was leaning against the windowsill talking to me over my computer monitor, I was quite conscious of my erotic response to her. Not that I was thinking of sex; it was simply a tangible, physical feeling, a magnetism, a feeling between my legs of the force of erotic connection and desire. I wished I could in some way express what I was feeling. Not in some ancient way of grunts and pawing, but in some deft, witty, modern (French?) way or with a simple statement—with a compliment or statement of fact. When Marta had gotten her hair cut, I had remarked on the attractiveness of the cut, and I suppose that on this particular evening I could have reiterated: "You know, your new haircut really does look good on you." This would hardly have expressed the nature or strength of my feelings, but it would have, let's say, allowed tectonic plates to shift ever so slightly. Alternatively, I might have said that I enjoyed her end-of-the-day visits, but this would have been a kind of putting the cards, or a few of them, on the table, making the subconscious conscious, and thus it could have led either to Marta's not coming anymore or to her coming more often.

Note that I do not want Marta to come to my office more often, and this because, since I cannot or will not fully express my erotic feelings for her, there is a frustration in her visits, a tension that makes the conversation stiff and dry. What do you talk about when what you're not talking about what you really want to talk about? Writing some time ago on a similar subject, I quoted from the Master of Revels of *A Midsummer Night's Dream*:

> A play there is, my lord, some ten words long,
>
> Which is as brief as I have known a play;

> But by ten words, my lord, it is too long.

The Master is referring to the backwoods production of *Pyramus and Thisbe*, in which Pyramus urges Thisbe to kiss him through a hole in the wall between their estates, and she replies crudely, "I kiss the wall's hole, not your lips at all." In Brookes More's translation of the *ur* text, Ovid's *Metamorphoses*, the beautiful, youthful neighbors, forbidden to marry, jointly sigh:

> "Thou envious wall
>
> why art thou standing in the way of those
>
> who die for love? What harm could happen thee
>
> shouldst thou permit us to enjoy our love?"

And in vain they whisper to the wall and its hole:

> "we are not ungrateful; unto thee
>
> we own our debt; here thou hast left a way
>
> that breathed words may enter loving ears"

By all this I mean to say that there comes a point in some conversations when one may feel that the breathed words—the sheer volume of them, is like a wall, which with each statement becomes higher or thicker, its chinks filled and fissures repaired, and all this to block erotic desire and to divert it with wall building. And one may feel, too, in one's loins, that a kiss or embrace would eliminate the need for speech. And then later, upon reflection, one may appreciate the sexual aspect of human conversation more generally.

To this I would append one of Ian Craib's observations in *The Importance of Disappointment*:

> I suspect indeed that the best adult friendships—with members of the opposite sex or members of the same sex—involve precisely these desires which are not acted upon. In this sense all our important relationships will be sexual relationships.

This might be thought of as a challenge to what my words above, about work relationships, are proposing. And so I, in my turn, would ask: If many of our best friendships and collegial relationships are born of not doing what we would like, if they are born of repression, frustration, and disappointment, what sort of life is this?

With such delight in her eyes and voice, and such an openness in her posture, Marta leaned on my windowsill next to the tropical plants, my gym clothes, piles of pages, laser printer, and recycling bucket. Unable to find a way to express to her what I was feeling, I was tongue-tied, and our evening conversation was at once stiff and short. When she left I had the sense that my tacit message had been something like "I do not have much to say to you, and there's not much pleasure to be had in stopping by to see me." Hardly an expression of my feelings! The present text is, among other things, an attempt at sublimation, at replacing love-making with a discussion of love-making that has not taken place.

It has been explained to me that in German there are two distinct words for "woman"—*Weib* and *Frau*—and that the difference between these two words is not the same as that in French between *mademoiselle* and *madame*, or as the differences in English between "young woman," "woman," "lady," "housewife," etc. My understanding is that *Weib* implies that the woman is sexually active or has erotic desires and interests, while *eine Frau* is often desexualized, for example by domestic responsibilities or her role in the workforce. (Or, nowadays, desexualized by the hormonal effects of birth-control pills?)

This phenomenon is not unique to German (nor to women working in Germany). Sticking just with language for the moment, I note that the Spanish word "maya" may be used similarly to *Weib*. "Broad" is a vulgar word that English-speakers might use as a substitute; another: "female." Interestingly, etymologically *Frau* has been traced back to a Proto-Indo-European word *prow*, which is translated as "master" or "judge." I will not be the first to note that a woman who takes on the role of master, either in a family or for an employer, may be desexualized or appear desexualized as a result.

The purpose of these notes is not to discuss German or language or the difficulties of playing multiple roles, but to propose more simply that in our work relationships, at least in the United States, men and women, straight, gay, and otherwise, are often made into some version of *Frauen*. Or, if you prefer, we are ever at risk of being made, or making ourselves, into *Frauen*. (Although we are more often mastered and judged than masters and judges!)

One might be tempted to follow this linguistic excursus with a discussion of sexual harassment. We could discuss how laws, regulations, and their enforcement have sought to remove sexuality from the workplace and from collegial relations, and this for a number of reasons to include because sexuality complicates relations between people and can make it harder for workers to work together "successfully." The quote marks are to call attention to the fact that in a different universe a rich and fulfilling erotic life (which is not to say one including sexual harassment) could be a key part of success, whereas organizations and legal regimes in our twenty-first century are more focused on goals like selling more cellphones, taking care of more hospital patients, or extracting other countries' natural resources and exploiting as cheaply as possible their citizens' labor. Let us note, too, that workplaces and collegial relationships have also become principal sources of erotic partners, of people to marry or to have sex or other kinds of intimate relations with. Although the erotics of the workplace have been forced into the closet, this closet is a busy and sought after location.

My evening with Marta came right on the heels of another, similar workplace interaction. I had been at a meeting with another woman I find quite attractive; but with "Rosemarie" I have tried quite a different approach, not demanding or even quite proposing that we enter into intimate relations, but telling her directly what a fan I was of hers and how, if she were single, I would be asking her to go out with me. While I had been pleased with the honesty of my confession, I had also felt that, understandably (!), it had complicated my working relationship with Rosemarie. We still worked well together, but perhaps not as well as previously. (And I need to say that while my direct telling may have made Rosemarie uncomfortable, it did not stop her from proposing subsequently that we start playing tennis together, though this proposal has not led her to finding any time to play tennis with me. It has been something she wanted to propose but not do.)

So now I was at a meeting with Rosemarie and several other people, and the event was such that it was only at the very end, when the meeting was breaking up, that I had an opportunity to appreciate that my colleague was wearing a silky black dress that made her look quite stunning. The next day she sent me the usual follow-up e-mail, and I set to work drafting my follow-up to her follow-up. My first draft began something like, "Good to see you yesterday, and may I say that your dress was really quite stunning."

No, I decided, this would not do. All the business notes I wrote subsequently would be colored or discolored by this personal remark, and it might seem that I did not take her work seriously; what came first was her physical appearance or my erotic interest.

So then I thought I would put the compliment at the very end of my e-mail, after the business remarks, but this did not seem right either. It seemed that in order to have a good working relationship, the personal and the erotic had to be left out. (It also occurred to me that in the past when I had suppressed my feelings—when I had said absolutely nothing—this had created space for Rosemarie to be more forthcoming. Once we had gone to the theater with another colleague and his wife, and I had not written Rosemarie immediately afterward to tell her (yet again) how much I enjoyed her company. And, in the absence of any response from me, had she felt a need to be more forward, to preserve or assure herself of my ongoing interest? It was shortly thereafter that, in an e-mail, she proposed tennis.)

Meanwhile, after the meeting and the stunning dress—the top of which not only matched Rosemarie's long black hair, but was transparent, revealing beneath a black silk camisole, which in some parallel universe was itself transparent . . .

I ended up writing Rosemarie a purely business e-mail, and feeling disappointed in this. This was hardly living life to the fullest. This was hardly being myself with this other person. This was hardly a reflection of what I would like to think are my priorities, in which not only erotic life but also frank conversation are supposed to rank higher than repression and behaving in a conventional manner.

Moreover, over the several years we have worked together in close, if mostly electronic partnership, Rosemarie and I have become, in some twenty-first-century way, close friends. Although we live in the same city, we have only seen one another once a month or so, mostly at group meetings, but have been e-mailing once a day or more. We often discuss, electronically, quite personal aspects of our current lives and relationships, our families, and childhoods. Even with our most pedestrian business communications we have made it a point to begin on a personal note. "Have you gotten out at all today? I had a great run in the park this morning." Things like that.

I AM SURE THAT THERE ARE MEN AND WOMEN who have found better ways than I have to relate to colleagues they have found attractive, and to bring more of themselves, including their erotic desires (their desires to be close to other people) into the workplace. I can also imagine people coming up with lots of advice and solutions that would prove to be "bad," not likely to lead to "good" relationships with colleagues. (These days other aspects of my work life often remind me of a line from the literary critic I.A. Richards: "It's very hard to overcome professional expertise. People's careers depend upon their having a say-so in matters about which they haven't thought at all." Plato's Socrates kept making a similar point about and to well-bred Athenians. And so I would say as regards basic words such as "bad," "good," and "successful"—we use them with a doubtlessness that is born of thoughtlessness.)

Decades ago I worked with an organizational development consultant, and though I had hired her to help with quite a different kind of team-building, at some point she commented to me that, in her opinion, sexuality *did* belong in the workplace. That is, she (an African-American) felt that in a successful workplace people should not be robots or shadows of themselves, but their full selves, sexual desires (or lack of sexual desires) included.

I would take this one step further. In almost every case—including writing essays or symphonies, or, say, making paintings—the work itself is not enough; it is part of being a social animal in dialogue with others (to include with others within one's self). If this dialogue is pinched or limited, if speech is blocked and communications are distorted or incomplete, this is a loss, this is less.

Note

Certainly the title of this short essay owes something to Eric Rohmer's film *Ma nuit chez Maude* in which, instead of having sex, the main characters talk philosophy and religion, the heat of their feelings well expressed by the tremendous number of cigarettes they light, smoke, and stub out. The film, released in 1969, forms part of Rohmer's series of "moral tales" in each of which a man, while ostensibly in love with some other woman, spends time with a second (or first) woman who he finds supremely attractive, and yet, or for this reason, he does not consummate the affair.

[5]

On Savoring

Some features of an ethics of tasting, good and bad

> [I]t is muttered that whenever any government wants to dupe the peasants, it promises the abolition of the wine tax, and as soon as it has duped the peasants, it retains or reintroduces the wine tax. In the wine tax the peasant tastes the bouquet of the government . . .
> — Karl Marx, *The Class Struggles in France, 1848-1850*
>
> It tastes twice the price. — An advertisement for wine, 2014

RELATIVELY EARLY ONE SUNNY SATURDAY MORNING I bicycled down the southern slope of Paris and across the Seine to meet up with a friend who lived not far from the river. As I was crossing behind Notre Dame, the streets and sidewalks were so empty and the river so calm, it seemed as if Paris and I were back in the Middle Ages, the water like a moat between the stone walls. Later that day my friend and I got stuck in a traffic jam along a commercial strip in the northern suburbs. My first reaction was to be annoyed. We would not have been stuck there had my friend, who was driving, not taken a wrong turn. I was looking forward to being back in the city, alone in a quiet café with the translation of *Robinson Crusoe* that I had in my backpack. But then I thought—we had traveled out of Paris to see another part of France; well, were we not, in this traffic jam in a commercial strip, indeed seeing, and not just seeing but feeling in our bones, in our frustration and dismay, a part of France?

I am reminded of a passage in Camus's *La peste* (The Plague). He is reproducing a page from one of his character's notebooks:

Question: comment faire pour ne pas perdre son

temps? . . .

Question: How to avoid wasting one's time? Answer: experience the full extent of it. How to do this? Spend one's days in a dentist's waiting room in an uncomfortable chair; spend Sunday afternoons on one's balcony; listen to meetings being held in a language one does not know; when traveling choose the longest and most inconvenient rail itineraries and, of course, remain standing the entire trip; wait in line to buy tickets for shows and then not use the tickets; etc.

What is this essay?

The present text may be thought of as preliminary sketches of a way of life: devoted to savoring. Painting the painting remains for a later date, or for someone who is a painter rather than a draughtsman. I would also stress here at the outset the awkwardness of this piece—the ways in which its various views of its subject will fit or- and not fit together. Of course awkwardness is commonly thought a negative quality, and one that a master craftsperson avoids. And thus an assumption of the present piece is that something may be seen or felt through embracing awkwardness and its juxtapositions, and this something may bring us ideas, intellectual stimulation, that might be ignored when reading more polished, or seemingly more polished, texts. This is also to champion, along with savoring, thought provocation. As if to propose that, if in our world the only product to which no one is allergic—the consensus definition of the good—is white sugar, it may be past time for some thought provocation, and for less refined texts.

As at a particular spot on a piece of drawing paper, I began work on this essay some time ago with this simple idea: In Paris restaurants one eats better than in New York restaurants, or, more precisely, than in Manhattan restaurants. This statement is not necessarily true, and certainly not true for all tastes. Some readers may have already begun disagreeing, recalling bad meals they have had in Paris, protesting that you can't get real hamburgers, New York pizza, thick steaks, or good "ethnic" (not French) food in Paris. New York water is not what it used to be—too much chlorine-and-pipe taste now? Only in certain neighborhoods do we still get the delicious (sweet?), naturally purified water we used to enjoy everywhere. But we remain in this more fortunate than Parisians, with their calcium-laden tap water.

Nonetheless, Paris's appearance in this text is hardly accidental. The city is the capital of a country whose people have a long tradition of savoring and of talking about what they are eating and drinking, and this tradition, along with the suitability of the country for all kinds of agriculture and seafood harvesting, has resulted in a cuisine renowned for the richness of its flavors. France and the French have been leading promoters of dining as a sensory pleasure, or as a series of sensory pleasures. And it is possible that French culture, being older and having deeper roots than American culture, has been able to better embrace new forms of entertainment—movies, television, the Internet—without entirely trashing existing forms such as dining. The meal in France remains an event in a way that in the United States it is rarely (or only on Thanksgiving?). Compared to New York (where I live), in Paris, or in an ideal Paris, one lingers longer over one's meals, one notes and savors more of the flavors of the meal.

Certainly things taste differently (and artworks, landscapes, and urban scenes look different) in a culture that is attached to savoring, or during those moments when we, whoever and wherever we may be, are caught up in savoring, as opposed, say, to being caught up in acquiring, or in worrying about our mortality (health) or our thinness, or in writing essays about savoring, mortality, or dieting. The present essay will also argue that even in the "best" Paris restaurants the savoring is limited; many of the flavors or aspects of meals are commonly ignored in France as elsewhere. "Social flavors," such as the taste of commercial rents or of the minimum wage paid to immigrants working in kitchens, will get particular attention.

In short, Paris has offered this piece a starting place, and readers may be coming to understand that I am not taking their time in order to remind them that they might eat better (in the sense of more delicious or healthy foods and dishes) if they lived in Paris (or, say, in Italy or Beijing). To the contrary. One of the features of savoring that this essay focuses on is how it can heighten our sensitivity not only to good ("tasty," orally pleasing) things, but also to what can be called bad or off, unwelcome tastes. One of the chief arguments against savoring, and indeed one of the reasons many people rarely bother with it, could be this feature: the less one seeks to savor the foods one is eating or the life one is living, the less one will have to confront the complexity of the flavors, the complexity of our interactions with the world around us, and the not always sweet or even healthy aspects of life that we are ingesting.

Life and my writing have given me many occasions to quote from Ian Craib's *The Importance of Disappointment*. The apt passage here is:

> There are . . . a number of aspects to [psychological] integration that can make it a not-so-attractive prospect . . . . It means becoming aware of and suffering conflicts; becoming aware of and putting up with what I have described as authentically bad aspects of relationships, and of the self; . . .

Similarly, I am proposing, savoring can increase our integration with the lives we are living, but this can include, though not be limited to, increasing our awareness of conflicts, of personal limitations, and so forth. Even if this essay were to limit itself to gustatory flavors, the discontents of savoring could be appreciated.

Americans have developed, or have been trained to have, a taste for bland and sweetened food. Thus Manhattan restaurateurs are not encouraged to offer less than bland (or tastier) food, and they may have some difficulty obtaining and may have to pay extra for physically flavorful meats, vegetables, bread, and so forth. If one is physically hungry in New York and seeks a hamburger or slice of pizza to fill one's stomach and send fats and proteins into one's bloodstream, the chance of finding a "good" hamburger or pizza slice—one that fulfills these purposes—will be high, assuming one has enough money to buy food. But if one seeks a burger or slice that will be pleasing to one's palate, entertaining it with some music of pleasing flavors and textures—experience has taught me that the chances are not good that one will be successful (and the price will be relatively high). And so what if one were to savor even in one's quickly obtained, blood-sugar-restoring burger a sense of limitation—a sense that you did not have access to all types of burgers? One could find oneself "savoring" (with limited enjoyment) mortality, or the not-everything-possible flavor of mortality.

Nonetheless, let's say. Plato's Socrates famously proposed that a life unexamined was not worth living. In a less heroic age this essay proposes that a life dedicated in some part, though hardly entirely, to savoring the life one is living could be a life well lived. (Why "hardly entirely"? Well, there would be a paralysis or an endless feedback loop in a life devoted entirely to savoring. Were I to try to fully savor the writing of this essay on savoring, how would I be able to keep writing it—and with what kinds of flavors and textures would I then be left?)

Given my belief that the ethical question—what should I do, at this moment or in general?—is not only central in human lives, but cannot be answered with any certainty, and given my belief that our thoughts and customs are channeled by our circumstances, prevailing economic systems included, it would be absurd for this piece to propose that people should live a life of savoring. What seems less absurd, and equally diverting, is to consider what a life focused on savoring might involve.

I note, too, that as savoring involves tastes, readers should expect to continue to encounter in this piece a plethora of tastes—my tastes, which may seem to range from the conventional to the snooty and bizarre. There may prove to be less pleasure in savoring my prose or ideas than in taking issue with them.

To savor

For the verb "savor," the Internet gave me the following "quick definitions from Macmillan":

> To enjoy an experience, activity, or feeling as much as

you can and for as long as you can. (Bill savored the view as he cruised along the coastline.)

To enjoy the flavor of something as much as you can by eating or drinking it slowly. (I sipped my coffee, savoring every mouthful.)

Mine, you can say, is a savoring that embraces more than just joy, or that, in seeking to take note of all the flavors of existence gives enjoying short shrift. Bad coffee, I am proposing, can be savored for its badness (wateriness? excessive bitterness or acidity?), and sad moments for their sadness, just as much as tasty mouthfuls or joyous moments are savored for their more agreeable qualities. We might think, too, of the Japanese ideal of *wabi-sabi*, by which beauty lies in the imperfect, impermanent, and incomplete. Scenes, objects, and experiences that are beautiful in this way can provoke melancholy and spiritual longing—which feelings, and the qualities that inspire them, worthy souls know to savor.

Mes actes font lever des valeurs comme des perdrix, Sartre proposed. My acts cause values to spring up like partridges. Except that, in our present pass, the partridges are questions, springing up each time we, exploring a field in a pre-dawn hour, extend a toe. Does the idea of savoring imply a focus on sensations or is there an intellectual form of savoring? Does savoring have to involve consciousness—of flavors, of beauty, or of the fact that one is savoring? Are some phenomena—coffee, coastlines, our sadness—easier to savor than others—the taste of water, motor-vehicle or inbox traffic, the suffering of others, ecstasy? Can questioning contribute to savoring? (I believe so.)

Taking a brutal detour, I must ask, too, what is the "taste" of knowledge about starvation or of an Internet newsflash—260,000 people died during a famine in Somalia? The World Food Programme has reported that more than 10 percent of the world's population—more than 800 million people—do not have enough to eat, and poor nutrition causes nearly half of the deaths in children under 5 years old (more than 3 million deaths per year). These factoids may make any ethics of savoring seem grotesque. (To say nothing of "Be happy!" or seeing the glass as half full or even Marilyn Monroe's sad "I know I will never be happy, but I know I can be gay!") If, in the face of World Food Programme reports and the many similar we could collect, we continue to explore an ethics of savoring, could this be with an idea that in a world in which seeking to pay greater attention to our experiences, *à table* and elsewhere, played a larger part—and making more and more money a somewhat smaller part—fewer people might starve? Or would this be disingenuous, a rationalization for a bourgeois text?

At an extreme it could be proposed that a meal should taste better if one eats it with the knowledge that other people are not starving to death. This would be, however, to ignore one of the less welcome, yet fundamental aspects of savoring meals. The deliciousness of a meal (or of a rare wine or a particularly fresh fruit, or of a Caribbean beach) often owes a good deal to rareness or specialness, with this linking to a sense that the flavors and pleasures are not available to all (or at all seasons). It is not far from here to the pleasure some derive from driving a fancy car or from living in a large house—the pleasure of knowing that many others cannot afford such luxuries. The relative rarity and high cost of "my" vacation home's view gives me a means of savoring how successful or lucky "I" am. From this perspective we need to ask whether the pleasure of, say, getting to eat good food (however goodness might be defined), and of having the time and relaxation to savor it, would be diminished if one held in one's consciousness the fact that many or most people could or did enjoy the same good fortune?

Excursus related to vegetarianism

I recall in the 1980s buying chickens in North Carolina supermarkets for 29 cents a pound (about the same price at that time as a pound, or pint, of gasoline). The chicken had no flavor and was loaded with extra hormones and antibiotics, and nor was I—an editor of a progressive weekly paper—unaware of the low pay of the chicken processors and the unhealthy conditions under which they worked. But there was an additional and not pleasant flavor in the meat—of a life (in this case, the chicken's life) being worth so little:

29¢/pound. Rarely when I was eating this chicken did I consciously acknowledge that the flesh I was eating was almost worthless, and yet I think that this chicken did make me feel diminished, as if my life, too, might be of such little value. And yet again, we cannot ignore, that chicken at 29 cents a pound can be purchased by many more people than the richly flavored, free-range *poulet jaune* one may order in certain Paris restaurants, or than the $3.99 heads of organic broccoli that have been for sale at my local Whole Foods supermarket.

And in almost every case, if we are to eat, other beings, animal or vegetable, must be eaten. An exception would be a milk-only diet, which would involve the exploitation, but not consumption, of other beings. And do we feel differently about eating seeming parents (e.g. fish caught in the wild or wheat) than we do about eating "offspring" who might, if not eaten, become parents (eggs, beans, apples)?

The various forms of vegetarianism now practiced often involve, among other things, a degree of ethical sophistication and a belief in traditional hierarchies. That is, for example, some people consider it morally better to eat eggs rather than chicken, or to eat vegetables rather than any fish, fowl, or mammal. This would seem linked to a sense that a chicken is autonomous in a way that an egg is not, and because more complex organisms seem somehow superior to less complex ones, as do those animals that seem most like we humans. So a savoring question would be: In practicing vegetarianism can an individual taste or even enjoy such values, hierarchies, and affiliations?

While I eat most everything, I am not without sympathy for vegetarian ethics, to include for the idea that more human beings could be fed were we all vegetarians or better, insect eaters. (Though, and while I would not have even one child die or even suffer much, I do not want all these billions of people. I would rather there were more room and resources for other entities and for emptiness.) At the same time, it seems to me that vegetarianism often involves various forms of denial, self-denial included. The essayist and child psychoanalyst Adam Phillips has written and spoken well about how frightening our appetites, our voraciousness, can be. There is only so much "aliveness" we can bear, and we are highly ambivalent about aggression. And thus, among other things, we fight—with our parents, with restaurants, with ourselves—to limit what we eat, insisting that, for ethical or physical-health reasons—or to "look good"—we must limit ourselves.)

The denial that I wish to sketch in this portion of this essay is the denial of the notion that eating involves eating: the consumption of an other. This other is destroyed so that "I" can live on. If we are interested in savoring our food or our meals in all their dimensions, then we should not deny this aspect of eating and of existence. There, but for the grace of those who in dying nourish me, go I.

For some reason in Paris restaurants oysters are much more substantial than they are in New York, and this plays no small part in the pleasure to be had eating raw oysters in Paris, and hardly least in the late spring when the oysters are particularly succulent. Many others have extolled the gustatory and tactile wonders, the softness of the flesh mixed with the saltiness of the taste, and the accompanying flavors of butter, lemon, shallots, white wine, and a sense of the sea. (We are not far from the tastes and pleasures of oral sex; or, rather, oyster eating and drinking good wine can be thought of as forms of oral eroticism, of savoring life and desire in one's mouth. And our enthusiasm for oral sex suggests how attached we are to eating!) In the midst of all this, let us not ignore how in taking our time as we eat oysters, in savoring the flavors, the odors, the experience, we are also in some way reveling in the pleasure of swallowing another being, raw and whole, in one delicious swallow.

In his twelfth year my son went through a bacon phase. He wanted bacon for breakfast every morning, and we had a particular, chemicals-free brand that we favored (for his six slices and my one). It was a nice feature of this brand that from packet to packet the thickness of the slices varied, and our preference was for the thicker slices. One morning during the time I was first drafting this essay I remarked to Jonah about this variation, which is unusual for a packaged product. "Perhaps it depends on the pig," Jonah said. This seemed to me a nice fantasy. We might say that the pig is lost in the bacon and to an extent that a raw oyster on the half shell certainly is not. (We will get to our version Marx's fetishism of commodities right below.)

Social flavors (and some snooty tastes)

In New York one of the great staples of restaurant "food"—or, if you prefer, of restaurant conversation—is real estate, real-estate prices in particular. As I was editing these pages over lunch in the gentleman's-club-like Gramercy Tavern dining room, a man several tables away said loudly to a fellow diner: "How much are you paying for your apartment?" In Paris diners often talk about the tastes and ingredients of the foods they are eating, and this often leads to memories of other foods they have eaten at other times. It is important to recognize that either conversation—about real estate or, say, old breads—can seem formulaic and tiresome, and particularly when you are hearing or caught up in it for the umpteenth time. Yet, as regards the taste of the food on your plate and of the wine in your glass, it makes a difference which conversation you are having or which you are likely to have. This is in part because restaurateurs will seek to offer different flavors to people who are going to be talking about real estate and to people who are going to be talking about the food. ("Voilà ce qu'on ne peut obtenir au cabaret . . . : une daube de bœuf où la gelée ne sente pas la colle, et où le bœuf ait pris parfum des carottes". Proust: Here's something you can't get in a cabaret : cold beef casserole in which the jelly does not taste of glue and the meat has caught the flavor of the carrots.)

An urbanist once explained to me that Parisian café life—the fact that in Paris one can linger for hours over a single espresso—was related to French tax policy, which led to ground-floor commercial rents being lower in Paris than, say, in New York. Even if this happens not to be true, a chief ingredient, if not the chief ingredient, in every big-city-café-or-restaurant order—be it an espresso, steak, or gluten-free pasta—is rent. And thus I am proposing that a true gourmet, a person with a great capacity for tasting the flavors in her food, would be able to discern the tastes of rent, and of taxes, of the cost of service, of human labor. In a New York restaurant she would be able to taste the exploitation of immigrants who do much of the kitchen work, or he could taste the fact that many workers feel compelled to come to work even when they are sick. In contemporary winespeak, a wine may have, for example, fruit aromas of strawberry and Bing cherry with hints of cedar, vanilla, and lavender. In the Marxist foodspeak of this essay, a steak could have aromas of the domestication of cattle; of agribusiness, agrochemicals, and genetically modified feed; and of refrigeration and the complex modern commodity distribution systems, with hints of property law and the role of capital in driving up real-estate prices. Clearly it would take a very developed palate to be able to taste all this, and such tasting might be easier in New York than in Paris, since the food served in the latter city might have both stronger and more subtle "physical" flavors, which would interfere with the savoring of the "social" ones.

I might go on at some length, airing my complaints, stating my own tastes, circling back to Marx. My mother used to put carrots in her tomato sauce to counteract the acidity of the tomatoes, but now carrots are often just orange-ish fiber, and tomato-sauce-makers use fructose or cane sugar instead. And the Francophile in me cannot help asking: If a self-respecting restaurant serves bread without a pronounced crust, wouldn't that only be so that we could appreciate, as with a brioche, *la mie*. So shouldn't this—the inside part—have some flavor besides that of sugar or corn syrup? Inoffensiveness is a form of offensiveness. One good French or Moroccan melon, or a good French or Russian strawberry, can make it hard to ever want to eat an American melon or strawberry again. The melon lacks what the French call *un parfum*, a scent; the strawberry, while huge, has a taste of tastelessness (or of sawdust?). I have eaten in relatively fancy New York restaurants that offer special, local, free-range chicken, which may well be tender, but has no flavor. I presume that this is at least in part because the farmers know that flavor—that is, a gamier or bird-ier flavor—is not wanted.

Chain restaurants and their names—chosen by consultants

with the help of focus groups—demoralize me, or deaden my pallet. I was once talking with a restaurateur friend about the declining quality of a chain of New York "Belgian" restaurants, and he explained to me how periodically the stockholders or bankers of such restaurants review the bottom line and look for ways of raising revenues and cutting costs. Inevitably the managers are directed to find cheaper suppliers for the meat, coffee, wine, bread, and this, in my experience, is all too easy to taste.

There is also the pleasure and taste of security, and of feeling—in a restaurant serving delicate little portions?—that our voraciousness, our insatiability is being successfully denied. If you eat a well-done hamburger made from meat that had no flavor to begin with, the lack of flavor may assure you (rightly or wrongly) that you are not being poisoned. Is there a related pleasure, too, in not feeling forced to have a potentially new experience or, in some sense, any gustatory experience at all? (And can this, too, be savored?) In a general sense, the insecurities of our current era may not be all that different from those of so many previous eras, but it may be that now, as we are barraged by advertisements and "information," non-experiences are coming to be a great luxury. I think of my son, during his "latency" period, reading and re-reading the works of various fantasy and espionage novelists. The plots all followed the same few formulas, good was always triumphing over evil, etc. The blandness and repetition seemed to be at the heart of the pleasure—soothing.

When George W. Bush was President there was a story, perhaps apocryphal, that he liked peanut-butter-and-jelly sandwiches with the crust cut off the bread. Were the forces of evil so deeply ingrained in his mind—or the complexities of life so daunting and disagreeable—he needed his meals to be as simple as possible? Once in Paris I had dinner with an up-and-coming New York fashion designer who remarked that he did not like any of the types of meat that I particularly favor: lamb, duck, goat—meats that have, or that even in the United States have yet to completely lose, a gamey flavor. Is my ability to savor so limited that I need robust flavors? Certainly it is easier to savor a gamey piece of meat than a bland one, but it is not clear that this makes the former superior to the latter, and even if we accept the values of the present exploration. Is savoring supposed to be easy? Is food that can be easily savored (e.g. raw oysters) superior to food (Budweiser beer) whose "flavors" (including the social relations involved in the production, sale, and purchase) are so much more difficult to taste?

American tastes are at least in some part a result of American businesses' efforts to take advantage of the economies of scale and of the efficient distribution networks of the United States. Rather than selling different regional specialties and thus selling the pleasures of particularities (as is done in France and some other countries), U.S. food businesses seek to sell one national product—one approach to bacon, one flavor of beer, one idea of pizza—to everyone. Even our ethnic foods are simplified, so that "Mexican" food can be counted on to taste the same from one chain to the next, and "Chinese" or "Szechuan" tastes the same in every Chinese or Szechuan family restaurant. The goal for each product or cuisine is less to please, tantalize, or surprise than to reassure and not offend. The "pleasures" are to come from other sources than the physical flavors themselves, which have been codified and minimized. Instead the consumer is offered such psychological and social flavors as consistency, low prices, and convenience, along with qualities that may have been injected into the products or chains by advertising. In drinking X beer, I may feel like the sort of character shown repeatedly on TV drinking X beer in the company of a lot of X friends and X young women in bikinis. (Let us credit manufacturers and distributors with the extraordinary insight that, if lots of customers and money are what you are after, the physical flavors of food products are best dispensed with; it can be easiest, cheapest, and most lucrative to advertise and sell products that have no physical flavor at all.)

Is savoring possible?

In recent years I have been spending a good deal of time in Paris—neither fish nor fowl; neither tourist nor resident. I have "my" room in a generous friend's apartment, my local habits, and my, albeit limited, society of local residents. At the same time, when I am in Paris I try—in a touristic way, in a way that I do not in New York—to savor the experience of being in Paris. I find this more or less impossible, or to be a kind of puzzle that I have yet to solve.

Of course there are moments, *éclaircies*, when the sky clears and details of the theater, set, and actors of Paris, tourists included, appear richly detailed, command my eyes, and delight. I have my favorite bicycle routes and places to stop and take in the view. Having lunch while reading, talking, or answering e-mails, I may be suddenly stopped by the complex flavors in a glass of good wine.

Perhaps the problem, the struggle to savor, has to do with our inability to stop time, and how easy it is to regret this. The pleasure of savoring—good or bad tastes—may lie precisely in this. It leads us to imagine that we can stop time—we are stopping it. It would already be difficult enough to "stay in the moment" were moments not, by definition, momentary. Approaching *le bassin d'eau*, the pool of water, in the middle of a French park, I am struck by the "civilization" of the scene, and I tell myself that I should find a chair and spend some time—doing what?—inhaling through my eyes this civilized quality and thinking, too, of the waves of mass murder that seem another feature of the European landscape? Well, the initial moment has passed.

I am reminded of stages in love-making, from together mounting the stairs (or taking the elevator) to tentative kisses, to more liquid moments and a kind of losing one's head, recovering one's animality, letting go and drifting dumbly into sleep. I would stop at any of these moments and stay within it for a long, long time, but that we humans cannot do. And of course the pleasure would be very different, and might not be pleasure at all, were the stairs more numerous or the carnality less brief. Often in a restaurant I will eat something delicious, or at home I'll have a little piece of Belgian chocolate with pistachios mixed in, and I'll find it so delicious, it seems I should have another piece, and certainly I want to. But if I follow my desire, the second piece is not as good, and a double dose of sugar will make me feel a little unwell and overwhelm a previous, so pleasureful experience.

It is also the case that, after the most wonderful or transgressive love-making, and often after the most extravagant or delicate meals as well, one may regret what one has done and not done. It seems one has gone too far or not far enough. Or one may note with sadness how the experience has been reduced to a memory and how far memory is from our initial experiences themselves. There may indeed have been brief instants when one was fully savoring, doing nothing but savoring, but most of what one retains—like red-letter dates in a chronology—is that there were such instants and when they occurred. "I remember that for a long time we exchanged delicious, simple kisses on her couch, and the warm wetness then waiting between her thighs." But this is literary and governed by the grammar and vocabulary our parents and others introduced us to around the same time as we were being toilet trained. One struggles, in vain, to work one's way back from language to what we would like to call the truer, more wonderful, wordless initial experience.

"J'aurais voulu . . . arrêter, immobiliser longtemps devant moi chaque intonation," Proust writes about the first time he saw a great actress perform. He would have liked to have been able—so as to be able to explore more deeply, to try to discover the source of their beauty—to stop, to immobilize each intonation of the actress, each facial expression. . . . But they lasted so briefly! Hardly had a sound reached his ear than it was replaced by another.

Ethics of the meal; noise and silence

Once in New York I went to a discussion and tasting of French wines. Participants sat at desk-like tables, and nothing but wine and water was on offer (though I was eventually able to get hold of some bread). Some of the attendees were taking notes, either for professional purposes or just out of habit—to give themselves something to do in between sips. (This was in an age before people blocked free moments by compulsively thumbing through cellphone messages.) All of us were paying inordinate attention to the qualities of the liquids we were sampling. And it struck me that in this way we were completely lost to wine, to its traditional role in society and as part of a meal. Wines have long been crafted to heighten our experience of certain foods at certain times and also to promote certain convivial kinds of social interactions (and also as a way of storing agricultural produce out of season and for protection against bad years, bad harvests). Now, in contemporary New York and many other cities, wines are also used, and perhaps some are crafted to be used, in this seemingly odd form of social interaction in which strangers come together to taste and learn. Of course many people who go to wine-tastings are also, as I was, interested in the social interaction and may be hoping to "meet someone"—someone who shares their tastes.

I recall a time—before we were all swamped by globalization—when French people recently come to New York would remark critically or amusedly on our American habit of asking for a "doggy bag," so that we could take home the leftovers. From the French perspective there could be no leftovers because in dining they were not ordering or consuming a quantity of food so much as they were engaging in an event—a meal, complete with conversation. When the meal was over, the experience was over, the only leftover there could be would be a prolonging of the experience, say, by taking a postprandial stroll or by recalling the flavors and conversation sometime in the future, in the course of another meal.

Let us ask what ethics this idea of a meal suggests. It may invalidate much of what has been written heretofore. It is an ethics of experiences of others, and with others, rather than of things in themselves. The strawberry, melon, wine, chicken, or oyster is not more sought after than, say, when kissing we might seek a particular color, shape, fleshiness, moisture, or saltiness of lips. Kissing is a shared experience in which lips certainly play a role, and in which the savoring of the sensations plays a role as well, but what matters above all is your relations with another human being, and her or his relation to you.

We can pause to complain about the noise of New York restaurants, a noise that now, like an alien species, has invaded Paris as well, and that is produced both by loud music and by the use of building materials that reflect sounds harshly rather than absorbing them gently. I once heard that shopping malls deliberately try to disturb their customers with music in order to make the buyers anxious, to make them try to soothe themselves with purchases. I assume restaurateurs have this in mind as well. As regards savoring, I would protest that, as it is difficult to feel two different pains at once, so it is difficult to simultaneously process information from two different senses, so that if one is besieged by sound, it may be difficult to taste anything but noise. (Restaurateurs may have this in mind too; noise takes the pressure off the cooks and lowers the cost of supplies. No point in seeking out the flavorful; the noise will render it unnoticeable.)

I would not, and will not, pass up this opportunity to protest more generally against the noise of contemporary life. In a youthful (1928) speech, the future composer John Cage proposed: "One of the greatest blessings that the United States could receive in the near future would be to have her industries halted, her business discontinued, her people speechless, a great pause in the world of affairs created.... We should be hushed and silent, and we should have the opportunity to learn what other people think."

But there is also a sense here in which I am simply being a curmudgeon. Both noise and silence can be and are savored. In the wonderful, inspiring chapter on music and silence that closes his *La musique et l'ineffable* (1961, Music and the Ineffable), the Russian-French philosopher Vladimir Jankélévitch writes about how, until recently, human beings tried to make sounds (music, conversation) to escape from their anxieties and the seeming silence of the universe and of eternity. (Now do we go on-line and use our cellphones, earbuds, movies, and television programs for the same purpose? Or would it be more accurate to say that such media are used to silence or drown out others and ourselves?) Jankélévitch draws an analogy with a traveler lost at night who speaks out and laughs loudly in order to persuade himself that he is not afraid. Thanks to the protective screen of the sounds he is making, the traveler imagines that he is scaring away the specter of death. But now, Jankélévitch proposes, this situation is being inverted (for the truly well to do or for some avant-garde, I am here proposing). Exhausted by the racket, we cover our ears, try to preserve our little gardens or islands of silence. Silence, rather than sound, has come to seem the safe haven. This, then, would be to say as well that—whether we enjoy the noise or seek silence—we are trying to avoid savoring, trying not to have real meals, not to have our thoughts provoked.

Savoring not savoring and patience

My son Jonah and I have our best conversations when walking somewhere together, and thus one of my top priorities as a parent (and having greatly enjoyed conversations with Jonah!) is to make sure we take walks together. And thus I noticed, too, and savored in a certain way, a morning when I walked with Jonah to school, and we seemed in no way angry with one another, and yet said nothing, just walked together.

Similarly, when I take the train between New York and Boston I like to look out at the Long Island Sound shoreline, particularly at the salt marshes between Guilford and New London, and at this sense of sea, river, and port around New London itself. But one day, caught up in editing a manuscript, I did not look out the window, and there was a moment that I became aware that I was not looking, and I savored this, this not looking.

I would note here, too, a line from Thoreau's Journal: "Nature is reported not by him who goes forth consciously as an observer, but in the fullness of life. To such a one she rushes to make her report."

And I find these lines, in Emerson's journal entry on a day he walked to Walden Pond with Thoreau:

> The charm which Henry T. uses for bird & frog & mink, is patience. They will not come to him, or show him aught, until he becomes a log among the logs, sitting still for hours in the same place; then they come around him & to him, & show themselves to him.

This is to suggest that something—the essence or close to it—is missed by those who try to savor (to observe consciously). Is there a way to begin in silence or to get back to it, and to be patient and listen? This would not involve the egoism of savoring—an experience on my tongue, of me in Paris (or Tuscaloosa), of me feeling relaxed after my yoga class or of getting my peanut-butter-and-jelly sandwiches just the way I like them, with or without the crust.

What remains?

It may be asked, here at the end, after all this discussion and questioning, all these sketches: What's left for savoring? How could it possibly seem a good way to live?

The argument or proposition may be summarized as follows. There would seem something—a resonance—in fully tasting, sensing, appreciating the life one is indeed living. A life lived in such a way could be a fuller life than one devoted to escape and denial, to ignoring and being ignorant.

I remember once hearing of a football coach who ate so rapidly and so distractedly that when his wife asked him, the moment he was done, what he had eaten, he could not remember. This happens to all of us from time to time. Much more often we cannot remember not the contents but the flavor of a meal—or, say, of a day spent at the office. We might say that the meal or day tasted good or bad and not know what we meant by this or have much of an idea what had gone into the dish. Busy, busying ourselves, preoccupied, do we, often deliberately, fail to experience the lives we are living? And is this not-appreciating something to savor?

[II]
Art

I saw the best minds of my generation . . .

who threw their watches off the roof to cast their ballot for

    Eternity outside of Time, & alarm clocks fell on their heads

    every day for the next decade,

— Allen Ginsberg, from *Howl*, Part I, 1955

[6]

The Third Man

AT THE END OF THE MOVIE *THE THIRD MAN*—which some polls have elected the greatest movie of all time—there is a sequence that is so blatant in its symbolism as to be corny. Soldiers, police, good guys, and bad guys are all running around in the sewers of Vienna. That is symbolism enough—humanity in the sewer. Along with the police, Holly, the writer of silly fictions, is trying to capture the bad guy, his former best friend, Harry. But Harry has a gun and has already shown that he is ready to kill Holly. In an attempt to save Holly, a young police sergeant rushes forward and exchanges shots with Harry. Both are hit.

So here now is the part that interests me despite its corniness. Holly and the police major have been desperate to capture Harry, whose money-making scheme has involved doing great harm to his fellow citizens, young children among them. But now, just at the moment when the good guys finally have the bad man cornered, they stop their pursuit in order to look after their fallen comrade, the young policeman. Harry, meanwhile, finds a metal stair leading out of the sewer, and, with superhuman effort, despite having been wounded, his legs no longer of use, he claws his way toward the light. We feel the life force in the man, the will to survive no matter the cost, physical or moral.

As movie buffs know well, Harry—Orson Welles—manages to get his fingers through the sewer grate, but is unable to dislodge it. The camera, now shooting from above ground, lingers too long on this scene, as if it were possible to overlook the symbolism of Harry's pale, fleshy fingers moving like the legs of an upended spider, sticking up through the black metal grate, helplessly fluttering, grasping at air.

I am not a movie buff, and my movie watching mostly took place before people owned copies of movies and watched them repeatedly on their TV screens. Still, over the past many decades I have watched *The Third Man* at least three times, perhaps half a dozen. I have appreciated many aspects of the film, and certainly did not miss the role and symbolism of the sewer or of Harry's fingers grasping at air (until his old friend, with the dead policeman's revolver, puts him out of his misery).

It was, however, only recently, watching the film at age 60, that I became focused on the particular sequence in the sewer—the good guys attending to their fallen comrade while the bad guy fights for his own individual life. I take my interest to have a corniness of its own. This is one of the lessons that life has taught me. The world is dominated by people—"sociopaths" is a word we have come to use—people who take little notice of the suffering they may or may not be inflicting on others. In the place of companionship they have found things such as ladders to climb on, testing their strength, exercising their wills, attempting to get out of the sewer.

Everyone else is in the sewer too. It may have been a construction of these "sociopaths" and their heedless striving, but the bricks have been laid and the tunnels and pipes continue to be filled with most everyone's help. What distinguishes us others, the less driven and alone—or what we imagine distinguishes us—is that not often, but occasionally we pause to let into our hearts struggles or dreams other than our own, beings other than ourselves. Our pauses are not long—in the sewer of *The Third Man* the young policeman was quickly dead and left behind. And yet these pauses may be the pinnacles of our human existence.

One of my mantras used to be "next to nothing"—until I saw that a cosmetics company had started using the slogan to sell products that, the slogan proposed, were wonderfully lightweight. From there we can jump to the old joke about the winning slogan for a "lite" beer—"Like Love in a Canoe" (i.e. fucking close to water). And yet—or therefore!—for a while I was able to maintain a feeling that "next to nothing" could describe my and *Homo sapiens sapiens*' standing in the cosmos and eternity. And the phrase could describe the *Third Man* hack writer's and police major's stooping to observe the passing of their young companion—"next to nothing." But, I would like to say, this is not the same as nothing at all.

OF COURSE HUMAN BEHAVIOR is more complicated than my and the movie's simplistic sketches. For one, very few of us imagine ourselves sociopaths; it is always someone else who lacks fellow feeling, and "my" behavior, even in its most unredeemable moments, usually has something good to be said for it by me (and, sometimes, by friends). I am interested, too, in opportunism. These days—as in ages past, I assume—there are many people whose behaviors seem greatly channeled by such opportunities as present themselves. If they are on the move and encounter two doors, one open and one locked, they hurry through the open door, giving little thought as to whether there is some "good" reason to go through this door, other than the fact that it is open. Thus, for example, we could describe Harry Lime, the evil character of *The Third Man*, as having simply noticed that he could make money selling watered-down penicillin, and so he did this. It was only after the fact, confronted by some former friend during a Ferris-wheel ride, that Harry bothered to come up with rationalizations for his behavior and made his famous speech about the masses of people being little more than black dots and the savagery of the Borgias having produced Michelangelo, Leonardo da Vinci and the Renaissance. (Apparently, during filming, Welles opportunistically added this famout line to the script.)

In my own corner of the jungle, in the offices and meeting rooms where I have long earned a modest living, I cannot say I have seen much great artistry or out-of-the-box thinking. Rather, I often see, and am often demoralized by, people who hurry through this or that "door" or into this or that betrayal of their comrades. They seem to be possessed by the great hope that their behavior will lead to a promotion. Or is it the fact of the door's being open, and other people plunging through it—this must be the right way to go, it's the popular choice. In a world that "I" do not understand, and am afraid that I could not understand even if I tried, I am grateful to have this sense of direction. And my gratefulness for having this sense of direction overwhelms any desire to wonder if my behavior has much of anything to do with producing a good product or offering a good service. Nor would I pause to wonder what such goodness might be, nor to wonder whether my behavior may unjustly harm others who may be a little less opportunistic. (Or who appear to be too dense to see open doors and to walk through them.)

Of course, the matter is more complicated than my brief description, because—no more than Plato's Socrates and his interlocutors, for example—none of us here and now will be able to successfully define what justice or a good product or service is, and who it should be good for and how, etc. We cling, as to a sewer grate, to an idea that, even though we cannot know what the good is (in general or in specific instances), still it exists. Somewhat like Socrates, the more reflective among us cling to the idea that there must be something good at least in trying to know the good or to reflect on it. And this even as we know we must fail and return again to the soil and the sea. (Next to nothing.)

IN A 1950 *NEW YORK TIMES* ARTICLE, the *Third Man* scriptwriter, Graham Greene, wrote that the nascent Cold-War setting of the film was just a convenient backdrop. He and the director Carol Reed were not playing politics; they were out to entertain moviegoers, "to frighten them a little, to make them laugh." Indeed, *The Third Man* does not involve much reflection at all. As my teenage son pointed out, were the protagonist not so resolutely naïve and unthinking, there would be no story at all. Like Raymond Chandler's Philip Marlowe, Fitzgerald's Nick Carraway, and many another, in *The Third Man,* the Holly Martins of Greene, Reed, and the actor Joseph Cotten sees the telltale signs and makes some sense of them, but this sense-making is post facto and in no way keeps him from plunging onward through seemingly open or half-open doors, and thus from one unhappy moment to the next, yet more unhappy one.

I suppose it would be too much to ask of the end of a big-budget movie to have the wounded bad guy—rather than murdered—handcuffed and led to jail to await trial by a jury of his peers. Holly's actions in the sewer were less his own than his actor's employer's. But might Holly have at least noted, prior to pulling the trigger, that the legal and perhaps just course of action would be to arrest his old friend rather than shooting him in the back? And at the end, he cannot even get out of town before he receives further confirmation that the woman he loves finds him of no interest, or worse. (She has let herself be completely enveloped by her love for another man—Harry, of course—as a way of not confronting her ignorance of love?)

Shot in black and white, written in black and white, *The Third Man* found great commercial success in offering shadows in the place of complexity, and basic human drives—what a Freudian would call Eros and Thanatos—in place of reflection. A Platonist could say that, seeing only shadows and allowing ourselves to be guided by our animal and commercial instincts, we will never find our way out of the sewer (or the cave). For this we must train our minds, our rational capacities, and our vision. History has yet to suggest that this approach is of much use, or that its light can do more than flicker faintly in some alcove, amid the instinctual, opportunistic rush.

[7]
Dickinson's Dying Tiger

I have proposed previously a first law of American literature, complete with a rider. The law: You are always going to come across one more, intriguing Emily Dickinson poem, ready to reward your attention. The rider: The poem may have something to do with sex.

Vivian Pollak, a professor of literature and women's studies, has found "anxious sexuality" in Dickinson's three-verse poem about a dying tiger. Citing Georges Bataille, we might speak more generally about how the erotic is based in a desire to lose oneself in or with the other—and in the fear of what this must involve. And Bataille may further help us by giving a male—and more twentieth-century French—backdrop against which Dickinson's brief fable can more fully engage our attention. A gloss and abbreviation of the last stanza of a Bataille poem: I drink in your slit and open your naked legs to read what kills me.

But—excuse me—in "The Dying Tiger" there is sensuality and mortality and even, perhaps, vulgarity, but no sex, no consummation, no communion either. The poem's two bodies, and two selves, never even touch, and it is this distance that kills the male and condemns the female to waste away (though she lives on with her poetry and regrets). The first verse:

> A Dying Tiger - moaned for Drink -
> I hunted all the Sand -
> I caught the Dripping of a Rock
> And bore it in my Hand -

We should keep in mind that in the poet's imagination the animal became a tiger, rather than, say, an ox, gazelle, or sparrow, though of course such animals thirst and desire, too.

> His Mighty Balls - in death were thick -
> But searching - I could see
> A Vision on the Retina

> Of Water - and of me -
> The beast wants only Water and her!

THIS ESSAY WILL MOVE RESTLESSLY between Dickinson's poetry and biography, on the one hand, and, on the other, challenges and feelings of our own, twenty-first-century lives. The goal might be said to be to collect all the water, the insights and suggestions, that may be found be taking "A Dying Tiger" to be about the possibility of intimate relations between a woman and a man. As I will note again at the very end, the poem can also be read as being about relations between children and parents. A third alternative: reading the poem in conjunction with Dickinson's biography, we can think about how relations with parents come to shadow a child's possible intimate relations later in life.

Consider the eighth line of the poem with its upper casing of "Water" and lower casing of "me." Dickinson often commented on how small, slight, and undernourished she was. "It would have starved a Gnat / To live as small as I." "God gave a Loaf to every Bird - / But just a Crumb - to Me - " (She was as in need as any tiger.) In one of her letters to the author, minister, and Abolitionist Thomas Wentworth Higginson, she described herself as "small, like the Wren, . . . and my eyes, like the Sherry in the Glass, that the Guest leaves." The great phrase, the one that brings tears to my eyes, is the last: "that the Guest leaves." I think of her father—aloof, often away from home, little valuing women or his daughter Emily, except for the delicious breads she baked for him. Among the things Emily learned was how—and particularly for a woman?—responding to another's hunger cannot relieve one's own? In a letter to one of her cousins, she wrote, "Affection is like bread, unnoticed till we starve, and then we dream of it, and sing of it, and paint it."

Dickinson's extraordinary literary output, the almost two thousand poems, can be seen as in part inspired by a ferocious desire to prove herself to the leading man in her life, her father, whose "contribution" was to take little notice of her, while he wrapped in narcissistic admiration her less talented brother. Certainly many

Dickinson readers, fans, may themselves have had parents who, the children felt, took little notice of them and their talents. More generally—travelling on the rails our childhoods laid down for us—many readers may feel not so much that God gave us crumbs, but that we, like Emily, have had more to give—be this artistically, intellectually, emotionally, or sexually—than there have been other people ready to enjoy and appreciate our gifts. And thus the dryness of the sherry left in the bottoms of our glasses. Tigers (and some fathers) are frightening, voracious—but O to be so fully desired by such a beast!

I have the sense, too, that, on a deeper level, many of us also feel that at some vital moments in our lives—in moments of passion (not necessarily sexual), and in our marriages, with our children or parents, with a homeless person—we have come up short. We may have left a feast untouched, or failed to bring "wine / To lips long parching / Next to mine". (And I wonder if this doesn't connect, too, to a false idea that the lovers of disinterested others— of self-involved parents, for example—at times develop. Even as we may have learned, again and again, how responding to some other's hunger may not relieve our own, we may also have this feeling: if only I could have really reached him, really fed him, he would have fed me too.)

In quite another context Yeats wrote: "Too long a sacrifice / Can make a stone of the heart." Emily's father distant in one way or another, she was left with her mother—"habitually complaining . . . subject to depression and hypochondria," is how the psychiatrist John Cody has characterized her. And, "emotionally shallow, self-centered, ineffectual, conventional, timid, submissive, and not very bright."

"I never had a mother," Dickinson is reported to have said. But this left her with her brother and sister, to whom she was very close. To borrow a phrase translated from Rilke, they became guardians of her solitude. As for her more distant relatives and friends—who might be better described as the people with whom she corresponded—many seem to have recognized that she was somewhere between odd, extraordinary, and "partially cracked" (a Higginson description). They struggled to respond, let alone embrace, her piercing sensitivity and linguistic gifts. Invariably they came up short.

Pollak, who currently teaches at Washington University at St. Louis, notes: "Her [Dickinson's] poetry was an attempt to keep herself alive by memorializing a range of feeling and experience threatened with extinction from without and within." Such a use of creative activity is hardly limited to Dickinson or to her poetry. If Pollak's line had come to me when I was developing my essay on Plato's *Lysis* ("Friendship, Deception and Writing"), it could have been adapted to characterize Plato's tremendous literary and intellectual efforts. Dickinson herself—in addition to bread baking and writing all the poems and more than ten thousand letters—she gardened, and collected and dried flowers. As Freud once put it, art—or creative activities of many sorts, I am proposing—offers substitutive satisfactions for our most deeply felt renunciations, and thus serves as nothing else to reconcile us to the sacrifices we have made on behalf of civilization. (And, I would add, the demands of this "civilization" may be felt in classrooms or workplaces or on electronic dating sites or within our families.)

And, meanwhile, the tiger—without and within—may well get tired of waiting for Water—and for us, or her. For a specific her—Emily Dickinson—and, more generally, for a woman whose own animal desires have not been desiccated and denied by external social pressures working within her. Even if something like water has, finally, been found in the rock, and even if the speaker is, or says she is, preparing for the beast to lick the wetness from "fingers going by" (as she puts it in another poem)—it's too late. The animal has died.

And, I hate to say it, but—in the nineteenth century as in the twenty-first—this deadliness, this missing of one another is the point. Dickinson even exalts it, or tries her best to. "The Banquet of Abstemiousness / Defaces that of Wine - " she writes in another poem. Or, in a letter to an older man who was eager to marry and have sex with her: "Don't you know you are happiest while I withhold and not confer?"

A famous French expression: "Le meilleur moment de l'amour, c'est quand on monte l'escalier." The best part of a love affair is climbing the stairs. The Dickinson, nineteenth-century New England version is:

> Inquire of the closing Rose
>
> Which rapture - she preferred
>
> And she will point you sighing -
>
> To her rescinded Bud.

From these perspectives, there is little point in actually getting liquid to the beast; the great pleasure is feeling the warm dampness come—and this while you are not quite able, or are indeed refusing, to offer yourself to thirsty lips.

The tiger poem was e-mailed to me by a friend who had heard it read out loud by a Yungian analyst in San Francisco. In dialoguing electronically about the poem with my friend, the following story came to my mind.

> Two people meet, and one of them would throw himself or herself passionately into a relationship, seeking to recover a more animal self or to lose his self or herself in love and lust. But the other holds back, afraid of letting go; mistrustful of the other's passion. Is he really that interested in "me," prepared to really commit, long-term? And is such committing, such a giving over of oneself, a kind of death? Is there more fun in just enjoying the lover's attention and thirst, and are we afraid that all this will fade if we give in?
>
> Worst of all—organs ache—while the lover moans and growls and waits, the beloved may enjoy the exquisite pleasure of denial, of denying another, of denying the animal within, denying herself. Until it is the beast who relents, gives up, and the possibilities of passion and of dissolving die. At which point the beloved alone may hold tight to her memories, regrets, and guilt, cherishing their poetry.

WITH SUCH FEELINGS IN MIND, we may be tempted to say that the third and final verse of Dickinson's tiger poem is more than a disappointment. The weakness—the lifelessness, the dryness—of the speaker's response to the great, lusty animal's death could lead one to find the whole poem weak, and from there turn on the posthumously exalted, beloved poet herself.

Twas not my blame - who sped too slow -

"Twas not his blame - who died

While I was reaching him -

But 'twas - the fact that He was dead -

Seen in manuscript, Dickinson's dashes are quite small, almost periods. I wonder if their meaning for Dickinson wasn't something like, "breathe here." In the tiger poem, the final dash, even when seen small in a reproduction of the manuscript, adds to the flattened affect of this verse. And what is the speaker here proposing through denying—that the tiger's fault does not lie in his voraciousness, but in his—a tiger's!—lack of vitality? He gave up just when water and woman were, finally, coming to his lips. We might as well blame him for ever having placed such hopes in the woman, that she might respond to his desire, his need, and not be distant and dry with him? (And be this in nineteenth-century New England, or in our current, electronically choreographed social lives.)

Or is Dickinson reflecting one, post-Enlightenment, women's view of men: that they (we) cannot help being weak because we are ruled and rendered simple by our appetites as well as by our inability to understand the more complex: women and social forces? Or have I skipped over the more basic point here: we're animals. The tiger's role is to capture others—with moaning, if necessary—and to consume them. And thus the non-tiger—however strongly she or he may feel a desire to give in, be consumed, she must keep her distance, approaching only when the animal is domesticated, neutered, dead, or soon to be.

A young female friend has been telling me how she is seeking "the love of my life," and this has reminded me of other women friends who have found such loves but only once and briefly. In several cases, the man died too soon after the relationship began. In every case, the woman continues to hold tight to a dry and fading self-satisfaction—to have once been so enthralled, so entirely taken by another! I find myself reminded, too, of the sales pitch for a contemporary book, presumably targeting single women: "My father in his coffin looked better than most of the men I dated." This is to suggest, in a sense, that the real tiger died in childhood, in what a Freudian might term "unresolved Oedipal conflict." Subsequent tigers are poor substitutes, and thus why give them sustenance, why respond to their desires?

POLLAK HAS FOCUSED on Dickinson's social circumstances, on Dickinson being a woman writer in Victorian times—depraved on account of being deprived—"unable to extinguish such inevitable hungers as the desire for literary recognition and for sexual gratification." Given her circumstances—"all the Sand"—how women were constrained—Dickinson was unable to satisfy such hungers either. I have no problem with this analysis, except insofar as it is only part of the story. If women—or middle and upper class white women—are undernourished and denied the possibility of seeking their own nourishment, how are "their men" living? Emily's brother Austin had a wife who was left out to dry—in a fancy new, Italianate home—while Austin, in Emily's work room, carried on with the saucier Mabel Loomis Todd. Anachronistically, we could call Mabel a liberated woman and propose that her biography—which includes her public career as a writer and as the first editor to bring Emily's work to the public and acclaim—shows how much better life has become for liberated middle and upper class white women.

But, again, this is a partial truth. Freud wrote of the sufferings and privations which a civilized life in common has imposed on *all of us*. We can read Dickinson's tiger as all of us, male, female, or trans, dying amid the desert sands of civilization, in which there is precious little nourishment—more "likes" than hugs or intimate conversations—our deepest desires rarely met. I would not say that these desires are specifically for sex; "communion" might be a better word. We would—and not just on drunken holidays or business trips—lose our individuality and isolation together with another human being, or with other human beings. And this instead of, for example, drying flowers, studying tango dancing, or reaffirming our autonomy-isolation in bed with a porn site, sex toy, detective novel, or favorite TV series.

When I shove social context aside and try to just read the words and phrases of Dickinson's poem, I can be proud of the tiger. He—alone with his Mighty Balls—has known and sought what matters in life: nourishment and love. I can even go a step further: as a male tiger he has embraced, even in failure, his role: to kill and consume.

But from this perspective, the female speaker of the poem is also doing her sociobiological best. She may long to be able to give herself over to desire and to another—or long to be the tiger, conquering and consuming. But in her present circumstances, faced with a hungry beast, distance and denial are her only hopes for survival. Freud writes, more generally, of the great common task of preserving ourselves against the superior power of nature. We now are less conscious of this superior power than we are of that of capitalism. But in either case, we might say, after *les situationnistes* of 1960s France: taking advantage of free will begins with refusing to offer up the drops of nourishment that we have, despite the odds, been able to gather. ("Le bon usage du choix commence avec le refus de payer." Decades ago I became attached to the following English variant: "The only free choice is the refusal to pay.")

MY SEX-LINKED EXPLORATION of Dickinson's poem is done, but before concluding this piece, I would touch again on two of the other possible approaches to the dying tiger. The poem may certainly be read as being less about male-female relations than about caring for or working around a depressed or otherwise needy parent. In a letter written a few weeks after her mother died, Dickinson wrote: "We were never intimate Mother and children, while she was our Mother - but Mines in the same Ground meet by tunneling, and when she became our Child, the Affection came." This is to say that the tiger poem speaks of another and still common experience: to be confronted, typically at a very early age, with a parent, or two, who demand more care than they are able or willing to give. At some moment or moments one may scramble to find and give something to relieve the parent's suffering, and thus also relieve one's own. But it's always too little too late.

A third reading of the poem could bridge the two others. As has happened to so many of us, Dickinson's relations with her mother and her father stained her visions of, hopes for, and experiences of relations with people met later in life, potential male suitors included. I will not dwell on the strong possibility, suggested by so many poems, that Emily's sexuality was more based in autoeroticism and homosexuality than heterosexuality. Yet we might say that the distance she so carefully guarded was rooted in a fear, learned in early childhood, of thirsty tigers, male and female.

To those interested in exploring such paths, I recommend the beautiful, heart-wrenching Dickinson poem that begins "I bring an unaccustomed wine". Above I quoted from the first stanza. I will close by quoting all of the first, third, and fifth stanzas (of the seven total):

> I bring an unaccustomed wine
> To lips long parching, next to mine,
> And summon them to drink. . . .

> The hands still hug the tardy glass;
> The lips I would have cooled, alas!
> Are so superfluous cold, . . .

> Some other thirsty [person] there may be
> To whom this [dead person] would have pointed me
> Had it remained to speak.

Closing Note

I wrote this essay before reading Wendy K. Perriman's *A Wounded*

Deer: The Effects of Incest on the Life and Poetry of Emily Dickinson (Cambridge Scholars Press, 2006). This valuable book argues that Dickinson was an incest survivor, sexually abused by her father or her brother or perhaps both. I read this book because the poetry had already convinced me that Emily had had incestuous sex with one or both of these male relatives. (Though I would note that "incest survivor" relocates her nineteenth-century life in a contemporary context.) After I read the book, however, my position both slightly shifted and solidified. Briefly here: even if he never gave her the least caress, Emily's father was abusive. He ignored Emily's intellectual and literary accomplishments while overvaluing her brother's. A patriarch of his time and place, he essentially imprisoned Emily and her sister in the family home, not letting them go out without his permission and discouraging them from entering into relations with other men.

I will hardly be the first to note that in the United States we are obsessed with, and indeed make too much of, the possible evils of sexual relations. Among the shortcomings of our approach: it can lead us at times to ignore other noxious behavior, such as how fathers and mothers—self-absorbed, lazy, overworked, or otherwise—may withhold essential nurture, interest, encouragement, love, discipline; any number of things. For some children such withholding can be as damaging (and art-inspiring) as "acts of commission," incest included.

A special thanks to Camille, who brought the poem to my attention, and to Gretchen, who discussed it with me as we machine-trained ourselves, side by side, at New York's McBurney YMCA.

[8]

Guston, Schapiro, Rosenberg, . . . Dialogue

Why do we think Guston made paintings like these? This becomes a question, too, about how we are compelled, how we respond.

> I think every good painter here in New York really paints a self-portrait. I think a painter has two choices: he paints the world or himself. And I think the best painting that's done here is when he paints himself, and by himself I mean himself in this environment, in this total situation.
>
> — Philip Guston, 1960

> I saw the best minds of my generation . . .
>
> who threw their watches off the roof to cast their ballot for
>
> Eternity outside of Time, & alarm clocks fell on their heads
>
> every day for the next decade,
>
> — Allen Ginsberg, from *Howl*, Part I, 1955

I FOUND MYSELF IN A PARTIAL SITUATION—or in a total one masquerading as a partial one?—a retrospective of the painter Philip Guston's work from the late 1950s and 1960s. This was when he was having a good deal of success as a member of the New York School of more or less Abstract artists, and before he again openly embraced the figurative, cartoon-like, editorializing painting of his Los Angeles youth. It was a gray afternoon, heading toward evening; the gallery's many skylights were offering little light; and I was in a gray-heading-toward-evening mood. I was struck by the emptiness in the large, clean rooms of this gallery, by how uninteresting, passionless, depressed Guston's paintings seemed. In a 1948 essay on "The Crisis of the Easel Picture," the then dominant New York art critic Clement Greenberg (not referring to Guston's Abstract work, which was just getting under way) wrote of how pictures were dissolving into "sheer texture . . . sheer sensation". Harold Rosenberg, in "The American Action Painters," his seminal 1952 essay on Abstract Expressionism, wrote:

> Satisfied with wonders that remain safely inside the canvas, the artist accepts the permanence of the commonplace and decorates it with his own daily annihilation. The result is an apocalyptic wallpaper.

While I would not associate Guston's paintings with "the commonplace," it could seem "apocalyptic"—and a kind of annihilation of the artist—the flatness and frightened imagery, the repetitions of colors, brush strokes, and patterns. We are not surprised to learn that Guston was someone who struggled with depression.

Before coming to the gallery—Hauser & Wirth, 18th Street, New York—I had read some of the critical literature, but not that much and long enough ago to have forgotten a good deal. For the moment I was a naïve, curious about my lack of interest in Guston's paintings. Could it be a sign that I was about to spend the next month, if not five years, of my life studying and writing about these abstract canvases and how rich they were? Fate might have drawn me into this gallery and this room, and my initial negative reaction could be to not wanting to always be fate's slave.

In her memoir of her father, Guston's daughter Musa Mayer notes how, repeatedly, he "abandoned ways of working that had met with critical success." I think our subject is—and that Guston's work reflects, inter alia—compulsion, both psychological and social (the extent to which external forces, often internalized and combining there with our native biochemistry, dictate our fate).

And compulsive work is both driven and disconnected, fighting off depression and seeking to slip away from the forces through activity. From Mayer:

> Something my father remembered the composer John Cage saying to him during the 1950s often came to his mind: "When you start working, everybody is in your studio—the past, your friends, enemies, the art world, and above all, your own ideas—all are there. But as you continue, they start leaving one by one, and you are left completely alone. Then, if you're lucky, even you leave."

Of course we can hear Buddhist echoes and thus imagine, or indeed feel, that the resulting work has a special purity or spirituality. And yet—or simultaneously—confronted with the work, an art-gallery visitor could also feel or see, less happily or more empathetically, distances—between the artist and his work and the world, and thus, too, between the work and the viewer.

Here at the outset, I should say, too, that I later returned to Hauser & Wirth, on a sunny day, and after having read and read—Greenberg, Rosenberg, Mayer, Meyer Schapiro, Roberta Smith, Eva Cockcroft, Louis Menand, Wikipedia. I had particularly sought out texts that might help me appreciate why the work of Guston and his colleagues had been lionized in the 1950s. And I had looked again and again at versions of the paintings available on-line, versions that, *grâce à la technologie*, deformed the work, backlighting it, making it more resplendent and translucent—almost as if one were holding an old photographic slide up to a light.

Surprise, surprise, given all this, on my second visit the work looked quite different. For one, the figurative elements in many of the paintings leapt out at me. As one may see faces in the clouds, so now I saw all the black, cartoon heads peering out through the forest of the "texture." Hammers, a wizard, chairs, a woman with a handbag, a ghoulish figure with a crutch, black and white faces together, as on the prow of a ship, a Santa's bag, full of presents, but not red and white: black.

It occurred to me, too, that in the United States—and certainly with white male police officers continuing to murder black men—black can never just be a color. Rosenberg had written, "The big moment came when it was decided to paint . . . just to PAINT," but an American artist whose palette includes black—and so much black—can never be just painting, can never be liberated "from Value—political, esthetic, moral." Monochrome painting, which became infamous when the Abstract Expressionist Ad Reinhardt exhibited his nearly all-black paintings, is said to have begun with the French writer Paul Bilhaud's painting *Combat de nègres dans un tunnel* (Negroes fight in a tunnel), 1882.

James Baldwin's approach to blackness in America has come to mind (and I would not be surprised to discover that Guston was as impressed by Baldwin's essays as I and as so many "liberal" Americans have been). From "Everybody's Protest Novel" (which is rooted in *Uncle Tom's Cabin*):

> The conundrum of color is the inheritance of every American, be he/she legally or actually Black or White. It is a fearful inheritance, . . .
>
> It is savagely, if one may say so, ironical that the only proof the world—mankind—has ever had of White supremacy is in the Black face and voice: that face never scrutinized, that voice never heard.

READERS WILL BE NOTING that the present text is a complex piece, moving between specific experiences in an art gallery and reading done in response to those experiences or independent of it. Readers may also be noting that I, like Guston and like his black figures, have a heavy head. The first afternoon, I found my way to a bench in one of the quieter rooms of the gallery. I wanted both rest and to try to absorb something about Guston's "Abstract" work that, naïve, I wasn't absorbing.

Among other things, it is a simple fact that in 2016 Abstract Expressionist work is a lot harder to understand in an art gallery or museum than it is when you see a painting in this style gracing the security desk of the headquarters of a large corporation.

Nothing better than an art work that speaks of human creativity and of being modern and with it and wonderful and pure, and without speaking openly about how organized forces are at work in our times and how human beings are caught up in the machinery. There is an extensive literature on how Abstract Expressionism—Guston paintings included—became a tool in a Cold War effort to win over the hearts and minds of foreign elites: writers, thinkers, and artists who remained attached to the Soviet Union, communism, and that now quaint idea: from each according to his ability, to each according to his need. I quote from *New Yorker* writer Louis Menand's summary of the literature:

> The theory . . . is that abstract painting was an ideal propaganda tool. It was avant-garde, the product of an advanced civilization. In contrast to Soviet painting, it was neither representational nor didactic. It could be understood as pure painting—art absorbed by its own possibilities, experiments in color and form. Or it could be understood as pure expression—a "school" in which every artist had a unique signature. A Pollock looked nothing like a Rothko, which looked nothing like a Gorky or a Kline. Either way, Abstract Expressionism stood for autonomy: the autonomy of art, freed from its obligation to represent the world, or the freedom of the individual—just the principles that the United States [claimed to be] defending in the worldwide struggle. Art critics therefore [and themselves subsidized by the CIA, et al.] developed apolitical modes of appreciation and evaluation, emphasizing the formal rigor or the existentialist drama of the paintings; and the Museum of Modern Art favored Abstract Expressionists in its purchases and international exhibitions, at the expense of art whose politics might have been problematic . . .

Naturalist art, for example.

At the same time, Menand notes that "no work reduces to a single context." Indulging ourselves? falling back on bourgeois habits and diversions? pretending that the story of our times is not like the story of the meteor that wiped out the dinosaurs, that it is not simply the story of capitalism's power and reach and insatiability? On my gallery bench I was open to many possibilities. Like many another, I have been a fan of the art criticism of Leo Steinberg, and like him I am open to seeing abstract paintings as—like a microscope—helping us see what is essential yet normally imperceptible.

But what—I am looking around at ten or so Guston Abstract paintings, to include, for example, *The Light* (1960)—what would, what could this essence be: our primitiveness? our incapacity—for intellectual, psychological, or politico-economic reasons—to make sense of our experience, our predicament? Marx (shoved) aside, could this *art informel*—Guston's seeming refusal to bother himself with order, beauty, seeing—could this be an inversion, as in a mirror, of the extraordinary human capacity to find order in the universe and to superimpose orders on it, to delight in our perceptive capacities? And beauty in art is certainly related to this finding and superimposition of order. And so was my seeming lack of interest in Guston's work an inversion of, a response to, anxiety provoked by his seeming disinterest in beauty, order . . . ? Or, in his best works, could there be found, as in the remains of a fire, the ashes of an anger that had once burned bright, against order and oppression? A recognition that order was a kind of oppression? "The difficulties begin," Guston once observed, "when you understand what it is that the soul will not permit the hand to make."

Guston's father, a blacksmith who had scratched out a living as a junk collector, had committed suicide when Guston (then Goldstein) was about 10, and it has been said that one of the reasons for this suicide was the anti-Semitic prejudice that had dogged the family from the Ukraine to Canada to Los Angeles. When he was 18, Guston/Goldstein painted for the John Reed Club in Los Angeles an indoor mural—not about anti-Semitism, but—on the subject of the Scottsboro Boys, the nine black teenagers who, in the 1930s, were being framed for raping two white women. The mural was defaced by local police officers, and I have also read that Ku Klux Klan members, who in Southern California were after Jews and African-Americans, defaced Guston's early, political murals.

IN THE HAUSER & WIRTH ROOM in which I was trying to pass to the other side of my lack of interest and to collect my thoughts, there were two other people: a young man who was touring the canvases and a woman about my age—early sixties—who was sitting at the other end of "my" bench. I could describe her as non-descript; however, sometime after a brief exchange we had and which I will eventually describe, I had the odd, unkind thought that she was a potato. A potato dressed as a human. (And what kind of unkind vegetative growth am I? A parsnip?)

I like asking people—strangers in art museums and galleries—what they think of art works that we are both looking at. It's a way of making a little conversation; it touches on my curiosity about how other people are experiencing the world, what their points of connection are. And these people's responses often help me develop my own. A Bakhtinian, I believe in "responses" more than in "my own." That is, "the unique speech experience of each individual is shaped and developed in continuous and constant interaction with others' individual utterances." Hence all my reading and quoting.

I am an echo chamber that has bursts its bounds, sounds, ideas crashing? Yet often I speak calmly, in a reasonably soft voice, albeit one with clashing overtones. I asked the woman sharing the bench with me, "Why do you think Guston made these paintings? Or why did he make paintings like these?"

It could well be imagined that questions such as this had been in Guston's own mind during the period when he was making these Abstract paintings. His daughter: "[T]he image maker in him that feared and longed to create golems probably never did feel entirely comfortable with abstraction."

On the bench, though, I was more attuned to something else I had read, decades earlier, in *The Essential Tension*, a book by the sociologist of science Thomas Kuhn. Kuhn had written that he did not understand Aristotle's approach to physics, to motion—it seemed to him absurd and of little interest—until he asked himself how a "sensible person" could have done such theorizing. "When reading the works of an important thinker," Kuhn thus proposed:

> look first for the apparent absurdities in the text and ask yourself how a sensible person could have written them. When you find an answer, . . . when those passages make sense, then you may find that more central passages, ones you previously thought you understood, have changed their meaning.

And so I was hoping I could come to understand how a once-politically-engaged, gifted artist could have made such seemingly aphonic or frightened paintings (or paintings about fear and repression)—paintings that, in their day, had seemed of great value, had been part of a euphoria, part of the United States' first great contribution "to the mainstream of [European] painting and sculpture"—paintings that now, on this gray day in 2016, seemed weak. An answer, or answers, might help me learn something about Guston's career, the art world, myself, and the "total situation" in which we find ourselves.

It has, for example, been said that the New York painters were trying to get out from under European modernism, the tremendous reputations and accomplishments of Picasso, Mondrian, the Surrealists, and so many others. And in this effort they could not help but succeed, since they came to maturity in the aftermath of the United States' triumphs in the Second World War, and thus when New York was truly the media and financial capital of the world. And, thanks to the Cold War, they had the CIA, the Rockefellers, the Museum of Modern Art, Henry Luce, etc., eager to promote their work.

The artist Barnett Newman (1905-1970) once apparently offered this, alternative view: "After the monstrosity of the war, what do we do? What is there to paint? We have to start all over again." (Guston: "To paint is always to start at the beginning again".)

And thus an old, mocking stereotype: Abstract Expressionist like child enraged, with finger paints, smearing a wall? Or making vague forms—the red pants suggested in Guston's *Actor*, 1958 and his untitled painting of the same year? Was Guston, passive-aggressively, playing off how such forms can, in our imaginations, propaganda, and sales pitches, and with some help from hubris, grow into extraordinary constructions, works of genius? All it takes is the chauvinism of a rich and victorious country eager to imagine—force the world to accept?—that it didn't just know how to make bombs and sell cars and cigarettes, it could make great art, too?

On the bench, my first hypothesis was that the abstract paintings were in dialogue, if not with propaganda, then at least with advertising. The artists were at pains not to make work that could seem to be advertising, that, above all, lacked its saccharine charm, its aggressive claims about what mattered in life, its reductiveness. This hypothesis led me to realize that the art historian and critic Meyer Schapiro had long ago taken this idea a step further, made it more encompassing. In his 1957 essay on "The Liberating Quality of Avant-Garde Art," he wrote:

> Communication . . . aims at a maximum efficiency through methods that ensure the attention of the listener or viewer by setting up the appropriate reproducible stimuli which will work for everyone and promote the acceptance of the message. . . .

And thus, by contrast:

> what makes painting and sculpture so interesting in our times is their high degree of non-communication. You cannot extract a message from painting by ordinary means; the usual rules of communication do not hold here, there is no clear code or fixed vocabulary, no certainty of effect in a given time of transmission or exposure. Painting, by becoming abstract and giving up its representational function, has achieved a state in which communication seems to be deliberately prevented.

Hence my puzzlement and frustration.

AND HENCE NOW, IN A NEW CENTURY, when in a museum I find myself wandering into a room of Abstract Expressionist work, I do not find myself pausing long before all the non-communicating brushed by the Absolute or the unconscious, these liberations from the object and from the demands of the past or of any future. Nor have I found these rooms filled by audio-touring or picture-snapping multitudes, curious to absorb or take something from, say, Robert Motherwell, Joan Mitchell, Lee Krasner, Franz Kline, Clyfford Still. And I assume that this fact—the flagging interest, this disinterest in work that ignores or scorns "the usual rules of communication"—is inspiring agents of the art market to organize prominent shows of Abstract Expressionist and related work, in order to try to re-inflate its value. (Another promising venture; the reviews I've seen of the Guston show share the present essay's broad outline: initial not-positive reaction which then gives way to variations on "given the opportunity to spend time with the work, I find more in it.")

As for Guston, given his return in the later 1960s to unabashedly figurative work—and in light of the figurative elements in his "Abstract Impressionist" paintings, as he called them—it could be said that he was ahead of a curve. Or meeting Pop Art half way? In 1960, in the midst of his Abstract Impressionist phase, he noted:

> There is something ridiculous and miserly in the myth we inherit from abstract art. That painting is autonomous, pure and for itself, . . . But painting is "impure". . . . We are image-makers and image-ridden.

This is an observation with a bit of fury or restlessness in it. In the explanatory materials Hauser & Wirth offered visitors, there was another quote—warmer, sadder—from the same period. For me it was worth going to this show just to come across this observation and, especially, its heart: "a loss from which we suffer." The whole quote, as it appeared in the explanatory materials:

> I do not see why the loss of faith in the known image and symbol in our time should be celebrated as a freedom. It is a loss from which we suffer, and this pathos motivates modern painting and poetry at its heart.

A statement from Paul Schimmel, Partner and Vice President of Hauser & Wirth and former chief curator of the Los Angeles Museum of Contemporary Art: "The loss of the object was catastrophic for the New York School."

This went along with a feeling I had had in two of the other rooms of the gallery. These were filled with large paintings (roughly 6' on a side) that were variations on the same subject. A limited palette of colors, a limited pattern of brush strokes, and the same large, square-ish black object: the same black head, bandaged or bound in one case; a well-dressed man's shoulders in another; a simple, heavy stone weight in a third. In *Painter III* (1963) it is a cartoon head—the racist, anti-Semitic cartoonist Hergé's Capitaine Haddock in blackface? And, lower down, we can make out a forearm, with the hand holding a paint brush.

Clement Greenberg wrote that "the dissolution of the pictorial . . . into an accumulation of repetitions seems to speak for and answer something profound in contemporary sensibility." Faced with Guston's canvases, we might speak rather of the unwillingness of the pictorial to die. Schapiro wrote that in Abstract work we can see "the track of emotion, its obstruction, persistence, or extinction." Faced with Guston's canvases, we might amend this: the track of emotion, its obstruction and its persistence in the face of threatened extinction.

Another rough thought came to me: supposing every night—armed by the afternoon's caffeine and nicotine, and this on the heels of the previous night's drinking and pontificating—supposing you went into your studio to work on the next one in this series of paintings. *A quoi rêver de se prendre une balle dans la tête*—one could start dreaming about a bullet to the head. From *New York Times* art critic Roberta Smith's review of the Hauser & Wirth show: "He [Guston] could not go on [making abstract works]. In 1965 he stopped painting, and did not resume for three years."

Much later, describing why, in the last phase of his career, he again openly embraced figurative painting, Guston offered a glimpse of where he was at during his intermediate, Abstract phase:

> So when the 1960s came along I was feeling split, schizophrenic. The [Vietnam] war, what was happening to America, the brutality of the world. What kind of man am I, sitting at home, reading magazines, going into a frustrated fury about everything—and then going into my studio to adjust a red to a blue.

Or, say, painting glimpses of himself, of the darkness in which he felt bound? Or we can think of his Abstract paintings as Rorschach-ish images that, in denying or only hinting at significance and meaning, awaken our longing for it? Rorschach-ish images made by an artist caught—by childhood trauma, or a desire to live comfortably? the art market? the media?—in the possibility of being an enigma, and that this could be enough for him to live on and others to feed off?

As I have worked on the present text, McCarthyism has come to seem, increasingly, an answer to my question about why these particular paintings. The art historian Stella Paul has written that the Abstract Expressionists were looking to make work "redolent of social responsibility yet free of . . . explicit politics."

With my "McCarthyism," I am implying that Abstract Expressionism was a way of going into hiding or of trying to talk in code, and thus to avoid being publicly attacked and blacklisted as a traitor (a.k.a. a defender of other interests than those of capital and of business executives). But at the time, in the 1950s, the politics of Abstract Expressionists and other *Poputchiki* (fellow-travelers) was given a much more positive spin, and one that should not be dismissed. Nor has it been dismissed, in the sense that these artists' "political" struggle—their championing of individuation in the midst of mass, bureaucratic society—this struggle is ongoing, never-ending, and may be seen today not only in serious and silly proceedings of many kinds of artists, but also in tattoos, hair styles, the championing of non-normative sexual orientations, etc.

As the cause of individuation underlies Schapiro's championing of Abstract Expressionism, I will let him make the case.

> What is most important is that the practical activity by which we [modern, Western humans in general] live is not satisfying: we cannot give it full loyalty, and its rewards do not compensate enough for the frustrations and emptiness that arise from the lack of spontaneity and personal identifications in work . . . .
>
> The object of art is, therefore, more passionately than ever before, the occasion of spontaneity or intense feeling. The painting symbolizes an individual who realizes freedom and deep engagement of the self within his work. . . .
>
> Hence the great importance of the mark, the stroke, the brush, the drip, the quality of the substance of the paint itself, and the surface of the canvas as a texture and field of operation—all signs of the artist's active presence. . . . All these qualities of painting may be regarded as a means of affirming the individual in opposition to the contrary qualities of the ordinary experience of working and doing.

AND MEANWHILE I—whose dilemma is to be an out-and-out individualist and—thus?—attached to dialogue—I asked the woman sharing the bench with me, the other person in this room at this gallery that was showing the abstract works: "Why do you think he [i.e. Guston] made these paintings? Or why did he make paintings like these?"

"I'm not going to answer that," she said. "That's such a dumb question."

A door closing, slamming. If you are going to hit strangers with questions, they certainly have a right to hit back at you with answers.

And yet, a door closing, and a reminder that only a few people—and they only rarely—want to talk about the subjects that I would like to talk about with my contemporaries. (And, yes, Socrates comes to mind.)

I think the woman may have gone on to add, "That's one of the dumbest questions I have ever heard."

In a world of blogs and selfies and people defacing themselves to try to achieve some measure of individuation, it is at best quixotic of me to expect much overt dialogue! These days, when I do find myself engaged in what seems to me good conversation—with people who are enjoying exploring with other people what they might in fact think and feel—I am often surprised to hear my interlocutors say something like what a restaurant hostess recently said to me: "That was one of the strangest conversations I've ever had"; or a young environmental designer: "That was not your usual lunch conversation!" I seem to make my way in the midst of people who don't want to talk or who are too busy to talk or who are more than happy to repeat to me what people in the media have been saying about things—political, entertainment, sporting, art—in the media. And they expect me to echo some pieces of this back.

Which brings me to people—Guston, Greenberg, Rosenberg, Schapiro, Schimmel, Kuhn—I've never even met. As a result of working on the present piece—long hours, by myself, in cafés and restaurants, surrounded by strangers—it has seemed to me that I keep trying, as for a dialogue that cannot take place, to bring together thoughts and people—often from the past, either dead or dead to my dialogic interests. (But, to adapt an observation of another great socialite—from Nietzsche's *Jenseits von Gut und Böse* (Beyond Good and Evil)—all this, too, is still dialogue!)

AT TWO POINTS in his "Liberating Quality" essay, Schapiro, thinking perhaps of works like Mark Rothko's, stresses a religious quality in Abstract Expressionist work, which thus demands "a sincere and humble submission [as] to a spiritual object, . . . [U]nless you achieve the proper set of mind and feeling towards [the work], you will not experience anything of it at all." I can imagine my bench companion not wanting her reverence for Guston's paintings disturbed. And certainly not by *un être humain* with so many thoughts and questions in his head!

Rosenberg: "The critic who goes on judging . . . is bound to seem a stranger"? From my stranger perspective, I have observed a vast country of sales pitches and smooth talking (lying and denying), to include by art impresarios, but—like Athenians long before us—we Americans are afraid of dialectic or of even raising the lid on the possibility that we might question our values or our explanations. And be they spiritual or scientific. The leftwing has its columnists who repeat its articles of faith, and the rightwing its columnists. A prominent way that class and group interests are advanced is by attempting to shut down (or simply not subsidize) discussion of alternatives. What is most politically incorrect or otherwise unacceptable is open-ended exploration of our feelings, ideas, and beliefs. What are their sources and justifications? Through what bedrock do these sources and justifications flow?

On my bench I was feeling shut out, tongue-tied, aporetic; in a room of abstract paintings, painted by a painter who himself was losing interest in abstraction. And then the young man, who had been touring the paintings on the walls, sidled over to me and said in a soft voice, as if afraid of being overheard, "I liked your question."

In Plato's *Lysis*, chaperones lead Socrates's young interlocutors away before anyone can say explicitly what friendship involves. Now a member of the gallery staff took the young man by the arm and led him away before we had a chance to really talk about Guston's work and about what Abstract Expressionism had involved. But not before I found out that the young man was in the arts himself, nor before he had a chance to give a four-word answer: "Because he had to." Why had Guston made these paintings or paintings like these? Because he had to.

WHEN THE YOUNG MAN SAID THIS, I took it to be a psychological explanation: Guston was driven—say, by his father's suicide or other inner demons or passions—to paint these paintings. It has been proposed by others that Guston in adolescence, in the wake of the suicide, retreated into comics, and thus became an artist. An artist who eventually came back to comics, as to his touchstone or solace—ever seeking the best means of escape from his total situation?

But the young man could have meant his "had to" as a social explanation. If you were a young artist starting out in the midst of the Great Depression, you painted murals, first for the John Reed Club and in Mexico with the help of David Siqueiros, and then for the WPA. And if you were an ambitious painter after the Second World War or wished to survive in McCarthy's America, you didn't paint political murals or other kinds of figurative work, you came to New York with a changed name and became some version of an Abstract Expressionist. Then, when you had secured a reputation, a comfortable home and studio, and when the country was in a more progressive phase, you might—with a certain daring and dismay—make your way back to a kind of work that had once meant so much to you, done so much for you.

I confess to being currently under the influence of *Eva Hesse*, Marci Begleiter's documentary about that sculptor. It gives the impression that what Hesse wanted to express and explore had little to do with Minimalism, but, when she was trying to become a prominent artist, Minimalism was a hot style, and some of her best friends were Minimalists, so she found a way to fit her work, somewhat, into a Minimalist mold (the synthesis gaining the name Postminimalism). If Hesse had lived longer than she did, she might have had a Guston-like moment. Become prominent, selling well, she might have made a more complete break from the movement that had helped her root herself in the zeitgeist and make a name for herself.

From this perspective, it is worth noting that Guston went to high school with Jackson Pollock. I can imagine Pollock saying to him, after the war and when there was no more WPA money, "Come back to New York and do abstract painting. You'll be a star. I know people who will help you." Become somebody you aren't? If escape is the goal, the good, then not quite being oneself is certainly one way of achieving it. But, again, this could also be why the resulting work—Guston's Abstract canvases—can be hard to connect to.

In her memoir of her father, Guston's daughter recalls him, in the last year of his life, being asked about his changes in style: murals-Abstract-figurative-again.

> My father looked slightly pained . . . "You know comments about style always seem strange to me—"Why do you work in this style or in that style"—as if you had a choice in the matter." He took a draft of his cigarette and paused to think. "What you're doing," he said slowly, "is trying to stay alive and continue and not die."

I proposed at the outset that our subject is compulsion, both psychological and social. With "social" here including political repression and propaganda.

SCHAPIRO WRITES of the Abstract Expressionists' "self-involved lines." Paul Schimmel, who organized the Guston show, said Guston had "spent a lifetime in a studio trying to find his own light." I certainly know the feeling, the compulsion, and I know how—in our conformist country, in our schools and churches, and by our mass media—we Americans have been taught to believe in the importance and sanctity of our own lights and of being guided by them.

And when our views and habits change—when we think how wrong or silly or ignorant we have been, or how beholden to market forces and fashions, teaching, and propaganda we have been—we do not think that *now* the times and the forces have changed me once again! We imagine, rather, that we've seen the light, a new light. Narcissus thought similarly, and thus was blind to his total situation, to the roles that light and his surroundings played in his particular vision—and played in the fact that he had any view of himself at all.

"The eye was placed where one ray should fall, that it might testify of that particular ray," Emerson wrote in "Self-Reliance." This may involve seeing one's own light; but it is first and foremost an assigned task. The eye does not place itself.

Must we—we Americans—lose ourselves in a deliberate denial of the external (and often internalized) forces that find expression, inter alia, in our creative work and in our ideas and feelings? I would certainly not ignore the economic forces, given how powerful they are, but—to close this piece at least—I will speak more generally of a dialogic force, of the sense in which we do not act, but respond (or, if you prefer, our actions are responses). We respond to economic forces, to intellectual and social ones, to the placement of our eyes and to whether skylights are, however temporarily, light-giving or gray.

For having broken out of the Abstract mold and broken free of the dictates of New York art critics and curators, Guston has become a standard-bearer for artistic independence and non-conformism. Nonetheless, when we juxtapose his own careering with the changing times in which it took place, the role of his "own light" seems to have been relatively weak compared to the fierce demands and staggering opportunities of his childhood, the Depression, the Cold War, and the Sixties. In the late 1940s, he, along with several other artists, was attacked by the Hearst press and *Look* magazine for his leftist leanings. For example, the *Baltimore American*, a Hearst paper, editorialized in October 1946 that these "left-wing painters" were "members of Red fascist organizations." These attacks were a response to a traveling exhibit which was to include Guston's and about 50 other artists' work—an exhibit the CIA had been secretly organizing as part of the cold war for peoples' hearts and minds. From this perspective, one must read at least with a smile a comment apparently made by Willem de Kooning regarding Guston's return to cartooning: "Phil, do you know what your subject is? Freedom!"

And as for "my own" ideas—I believe the present piece gives plenty of evidence that—like all of us, I am proposing—I am a sort of conduit or switchboard, relaying things read and heard from others and inspired by others' comments and even by their refusal to engage in dialogue. As with electrical wires, does my—or does Guston's—resistance to, or our processing of, ideas and feelings generate some heat and light that could be called our own? Certainly. This, you might say, is a human being's personal contribution to the total situation, the total network, cosmic as well as Earth-bound, in which we find ourselves enmeshed.

Why do we think Guston made paintings like the more or less Abstract works that I happened to find on exhibit at Hauser & Wirth? Because he had to—his subjection, let's call it, blackening his self-image and dimming his own enthusiasm for the work. If we ourselves, having fought our way to this point, feel a certain euphoria, it may stem in part from the escape compulsive activity offers and in part from an appreciation that Guston was doing the best he could, under the circumstances, his circumstances, to whisper and shout to us about all this.

Note: *The original version of this essay, published in* Zeteo *(zeteojournal.com), had, for better or worse, 49 footnotes, running a total of 3,538 words. Readers may find all this commentary on-line, along with the many bibliographic references, by Googling the essay title. The show was:* Philip Guston, Painter, 1957-1967, *Hauser & Wirth, New York, 26 April & 29 July 2016.*

[9]
Collage, TV President, Bonnard, Miró

IN THE AFTERMATH OF TRUMP'S ELECTION, artists and writers have had the feeling that all is changed, and their work, too, has to change somehow; they—we—have to come up with an effective response. One way I have approached this is, in my museum wanderings, to see which works from the past seem most right to me now. My two top choices from the modern-art galleries: Pierre Bonnard's portrait of himself as a boxer (which he wasn't) and Joan Miró's *Ceci est la couleur de mes rêves* (This is the color of my dreams). The current piece will, inter alia, present some rational explanations for these choices, while not losing sight of the fact that my choices were not made rationally, but instinctively, emotionally. (Readers can find on-line photographs of these two paintings and of other works discussed below.)

Both works have a quiet. This is most welcome, central. I keep coming across lines from World-War-era writers—Wittgenstein, Némirovsky—writers particularly threatened because of their Jewishness—what they are seeking above all is an inner peace, a break from the anxiety of being a Jew or in the minority, different. Feeling threatened now by the rise of neo-fascism and by all that surrounds it—the end of the literacy that reigned from Gutenberg to Zuckerberg? the relentless advertising, chatter, and spectacle, to include of art—quiet has come to seem precious.

And yet neither Bonnard's nor Miró's painting lacks for politics, emotion, or ideas. As regards Miró's work, from 1925, there is its little gray-blue smudge of hand-mixed color toward the bottom of the canvas, subservient to the more elegant "Photo" (technology, change, progress). Art historian Gayle Rodda Kurtz, a reader of drafts of the present piece, put the matter this way: "When I look at the word 'Photo' in the Miró, I think of the sadness for artists when the ascent of photography took away the major *raison d'être* of painting. . . . Miró's "dreams are the color of the sky, no longer in need of painting. And the word itself flattens the canvas—no longer in need of 3-D" or shadow or depth.

Miró's work is a humble or humbled plea not only for painting, but also for dreams and emotion (color), and for the beautiful essential amid or beneath the darkness, however strong or eloquent, of the now. The urging not to lose sight of our dreams dovetails with something I wrote long before Trump's ascendance—how in the last fifty years Americans and Russians have lost touch with their dreams for their countries, and a country and human beings may not be able to survive without dreams.

I would also ask art lovers: Would Miró's painting or his dreams feel too naked without the word "Photo" (and the seeming colon created by the script?) at the top? Would it not be twentieth-century art without this seeming intellectual something stage-managing the purely visual and emotional, the little gray-blue smudge of dreams? Preparing the way for the next segment of this text, we can also note that Miró's work hints at how, within a few decades, the re-presentation of images, with the aid of photographic and other processes, would come to commandeer the stage of contemporary art.

It is sad, too, that in our sophisticated times an artist can only speak ironically of his dreams. And it is sad that to see the color of Miró's dreams—that in order to see this painting—we now have to go to a museum that has rebranded itself with the name of one of its board members, David H. Koch, whose prominent donations to prominent cultural institutions dovetail with his buying of Congressmen and Congresswomen in the hopes that they will get rid of Social Security and ignore global warming. We might say that Bonnard understood better than Miró how our dreams are discolored by our bruises. The earnest, caring, art-loving individual—or the person who is indeed different and alone, not part of a self-interested, self-defining faction fighting for its rights or share of the pie—the individual puts up his or her dukes knowing full well that the bullies and factions of the world are going to knock him down, beat him to a pulp.

Voilà un premier aperçu du séjour, as Beckett put it in *Le Dépeupleur* (*The Lost Ones*). A first view of the resort in which we find ourselves, let's call it.

THE SECOND VIEW may seem to take us far afield. I am going to write about quite another set of art works, which were brought to my attention by a 2017 show, *The Ends of Collage*, at the Luxembourg & Dayan art galleries in New York and London. At a press preview, I spoke with the curator, who noted that there was a dialogue between the work and success of many of the show's artists, who came to prominence in the 1980s, and the politics—Thatcherism and Reaganism—of those times. My question then:

> What kind of art would suit, in whatever way, the current Brexit-Trump-Koch-Brothers time?

The present piece began as a response to that question, and I take my "answer"—Bonnard's *boxeur*, Miró's dreams, and non-pop-art—to be a kind of wishful thinking. That is, I see myself as attempting to deny that the kind of art work and artists who will now come to the fore will in fact be quite other than I wish they would be.

Art has become—perhaps above all and hardly just recently—a business—a means of storing and increasing wealth, of moving it surreptitiously across international borders, of avoiding taxes and ensuring against inflation. The poet Kenneth Goldsmith proposed that the art itself—from Duchamp to Warhol to Sherrie Levine—is a chronicle of thieving and stealing. A large, prominent piece at the 2017 Whitney Biennial called attention to comments that investment banker and Museum of Modern Art Trustee Laurence D. Fink had made at a conference in 2015:

> Historically gold was a great instrument for storing of wealth. Gold has lost its luster and there's other mechanisms in which you can store wealth that are inflation-adjusted. The two greatest stores of wealth internationally today is contemporary art … and I don't

mean that as a joke, I mean that as a serious asset class. And two, the other store of wealth today is apartments in Manhattan, apartments in Vancouver, in London.

We can think of artists as being paid to produce a more sophisticated form of gold ingot. Superior to gold insofar as each work is so individually marked and documented that thievery is discouraged; resale is too difficult and unrewarding. From this perspective, however, the drawback of art is that gallery and museum directors, curators and scholars have to be paid, in one way or another, to keep praising the work and maintaining its prominence. Otherwise the gold bars may turn to tin or dust.

All this to say (in part) that the *Collage* show may have been conceived as a way of calling renewed attention to the work of certain artists, specifically to American artists who have been classed as members of the "Pictures Generation"—e.g. Sherrie Levine, Richard Prince, and Cindy Sherman—and to John Stezaker, who has been doing similar work in England. The chief task of the curator is to develop an intellectual argument for the renewed attention. For *The Ends of Collage*, the curator, Yuval Etgar, a doctoral candidate in Contemporary Art History and Theory at Oxford, proposed that the contemporary artists cited just above and some others had, in the 1970s, given new life to the collage form. Instead of hanging back with the cut-and-paste approach of Braque, Picasso, and their associates, Pictures artists had found inspiration in Duchamp's re-presentation of a cheap postcard of the Mona Lisa with a mustache, beard, and clever-vulgar title, and in how Magritte re-presented found images in quizzical, thought-provoking ways. Thus, for example, the show includes Levine's reductions of Cézanne's landscapes to digitized color matrices.

While Prince got more wall space than any other artist, the show did not include the *Cowboy* "re-photograph" that cemented his reputation and once set a record ($1.2 million in 2005) for the most financially valuable contemporary photograph in the world. This work involved photographing a photograph used in a Marlboro cigarette ad, stripping out all the text, and framing the new picture in the manner of fine art.

Clearly, in the midst of our present predicament (Trump, the Koch brothers, fake news, and more), my eye and heart have found more sustenance in the Bonnard and Miró paintings than in Prince's work. I would not ignore that Bonnard in particular exemplifies the artist (or writer, scientist, etc.) who uses his or her work to block out most everything going on both beyond the walls of his comfortable home and garden, and even to some extent within. Two world wars and a holocaust, economic booms and depression, the invention of the airplane—such things are present in Bonnard's work only because of their unfailing absence. "Oeuvre d'art : un arrêt du temps," Bonnard famously proposed. Work of art: a stopping of time. "Il ne s'agit pas de peindre la vie, mais de rendre vivante la peinture." It is not a matter of painting life, but of bringing painting to life. As if it might substitute for all too gruesome, frightening, shameful reality.

Coming back to Prince, *Cowboy*, and the Pictures Generation artists (among many, many others), it can be said, too, that, child of New England that I am, I have puritanical concerns about work that, from one perspective, immerses us yet deeper in the morass of advertising and pop culture and that, to adapt a remark of James Baldwin's, presents to us the myths (e.g. a handsome cowboy on uninhabited plains) instead of the massacres. (I leave to readers to decide whether the massacre in Prince's case is of cigarette smokers or of the American Indians. Although there is much debate about the specific figures, I think it fair to say that we Europeans, in our invasion of the territory that became the continental United States, killed people and "ethnically cleansed" this territory—an area just shy of 3 million square miles—more thoroughly than the Holocaust did.)

Of course in making *Cowboy* and related artworks, Prince's stance has been ironic and critical. He might be said to be calling attention to how we have made a legend out of a massacre, "to reassure us that no crime was committed," as Baldwin puts it. And yet, again, isn't there a level at which Prince's image is indeed reassuring and serves not just as a re-photographing, but also a re-championing, and perhaps not so much of the cowboy and American individualism and self-reliance as of the genius and glamour of advertising? I can well imagine that executives at Philip Morris were pleased to see one of their images prominently featured in art museums, and I can imagine, too, that the art world and its public were pleased that Prince was offering them work—unlike Bonnard's weak boxer or Miró's quirky painting—that they could easily relate to. Precisely because the work, however critical, was also well-known advertising for a prominent consumer brand. (Similarly Sherman and Stezaker have re-presented images from the movies. The artists' own stances are complex, but the images remain images from popular movies.)

WE ARE STUPEFIED AND HORRIFIED by a President who gets all his ideas from watching television and none from government employees, scientists, and others whose careers have been devoted to studying contemporary phenomena in greater depth than journalists can. And, at the same time, we have come to expect contemporary artists not to look directly at themselves and the human predicament or at the color of their dreams, but to re-present to us the slick, two-dimensional images of people and dreams that are offered by popular culture, through advertising, movies, television, and social media. (Etgar writes of "the historical seam between pictures and images, between manual craft and the mediated reality of our time.")

Recently I came home to find my teenage son watching some crime drama on our big-screen TV. Like all crime dramas, it was not so much about crime as about relationships between coworkers, and I take the underlying questions—how do people relate, how should they relate, how do they get into bed together and what do they do there—to be a chief source of my son's interest in this show. It included a gay couple, an interracial couple, and two fitness-club-bodied whites, male and female, who, when I arrived, were about to jump into bed together. Even before they stripped down to their product-placement underwear and moved toward the bed, we knew they were going to have sex because a pop-music song began playing. The sex was a choreographed dance, set to music. And the choreography was not based on some exploration of how two, specific, three-dimensional people might have sex; the task for the choreographer and the dancers was to reproduce for the camera a dance that recalled previous hit dances involving actors acting out having sex in movies and on television.

With all the brave futility of Bonnard's boxer I urged my son to turn off the television, not to watch such things, to allow himself to learn about sex, and however awkwardly, in the company of another warm, three-dimensional human being. If you find you want to touch her or him in a certain way, try this, and see and feel the responses, and keep responding in your turn. I love you, Jonah. There is no such love on television, in the movies, in advertisements, on social media, or even in art museums.

IN THIS AGE OF TWITTER and of people doing more writing than skimming, I am trying (largely unsuccessfully) to keep my essays short. So just one more note before signing off. There are, of course, tons of artists, and some of them quite successful, who are doing work that does not play off popular culture and its gadgetry. One who comes to mind is the extraordinary Belgian sculptor Berlinde De Bruyckere. Last September at New York's Skoto gallery I happened upon some beautiful birds that a less well-known, American artist, Katherine Taylor, had made in a Braque-Picasso-collage way. She had cut and pasted brown scrap paper, the remains of discarded drawings, still containing a few charcoal lines. It did not seem to me that anything could be more perfect than her *Bird II* (also glimpsable on-line). There was nurture in the fact that the work—like homemade bread—had been assembled by two human hands working alone with simple materials. (A contrast, from Sol Lewitt, "Paragraphs on Conceptual Art," first published in *Artforum* in 1967: 'When an artist uses a conceptual form of art, it means that all of the planning and decisions are made beforehand and the execution is a perfunctory affair. The idea becomes a machine that makes the art.")

Manual craft gets my vote. And the bird was unique; she had

a personality and autonomy that Prince's cowboys—or, say, Levine's Cézanne-derived matrices—could never have. A critic might say that this was an impossible autonomy, akin to Bonnard's impotent boxer or Miró's framed, purchased, Koch-museum hung dreams.

[III]
Sex

Orgasm is the only moment when you can't cheat life?
— Question asked of Eve Democracy in Jean-Luc Godard's *Sympathy for the Devil* (or *1 + 1*)

[10]

Carol, Rooney! Smoking? Gun

"Entertainment" is an unsatisfactory word for all that Carol *makes possible*

A friend (not!), Ken, writes —

I HAVE A RIDICULOUS FRIEND. I don't know why I go to the movies with him. *Carol*—the closing credits haven't even started rolling and he says, not whispers, "Why didn't they dilate her pupils?"

"Whose pupils?"

"Rooney Mara—Therese's. She's supposed to be sexually attracted to Cate Blanchett—Carol—and her pupils are pinpricks, BB pellets. Is everybody these days so caught up in making movies and watching movies they don't know how a human body reacts when it's attracted to another person? They couldn't have done a little Photoshopping or put some drops in her eyes like at the eye doctor's?"

A beefy man leans over from the row behind us. His wife isn't happy. Could we please shut up?

That sort of thing only makes Steven, my friend, raise his voice, as if his questions were for the whole audience—people who, instead of fielding questions, are eager to applaud, thanking Hollywood for this wonderful film.

Steve, incorrigible: "There's so much chemistry in the script, there was none left for the actors or the make-up department? They had layered dust and water spots on the car's windshield for god's sake. It's not like they weren't paying attention to detail."

"Maybe there was a clause in Mara's contract: no drops," I whisper. "Maybe her agent said, 'You can play a lesbian. You *should* play a lesbian. But you can't give male viewers the impression that you might, in fact, be attracted to women. Maybe there *was* Photoshopping—to get those pinpricks."

"OK, then. So—in the sex scene—we see *her breasts*. Were those her real breasts?"

The beefy man claps one hand on Steve's shoulder and another on mine. It's as if he wants to crush us, but what he says is: "Those were very nice breasts."

Steven twists in his seat to face him. "Yes, sure, of course, very nice breasts, and discreet nipples, should we call them?"

The man is shaking his head and pushing his wife quickly ahead of him down the aisle away from us. Steven's words are bouncing off the man's distressed suede jacket. "But when was the last time you saw 'not nice breasts'—whatever they may be—in a Hollywood movie?"

Target gone, Steve turns back to me. "Every Hollywood producer knows, Ken, that if you're going to show breasts, they need to be a certain size and shape. The specifics vary decade to decade, but what doesn't vary is that the producers have files full of nice breasts, complete with prices and how easy they are to work with."

"So go home and watch some of Mara's previous movies. See how they compare. The breasts, I mean."

"Unless," he says—

"What, another clause in her contract—you have to use the same breasts they used for me in my previous pictures?"

"You have to admit it makes sense," he says. And I am pleased that we've made it out to the street, to the fresh air, and without someone backing us up against a wall, putting a hand to Steve's throat.

Not that he has run out of questions. "So why didn't we get to see Blanchett's breasts? In the theater, watching the scene, I was thinking, well, she's getting a bit long in the tooth—

"Don't tell me—there's a clause in her contract."

"Well, maybe there is. But then I'm thinking, if Rooney gets to use *her* regular body double, surely Cate can use hers. And when she goes down on Rooney—head diving between her legs—all we see is her wig, so there's no problem there. Just put that wig on someone else's head, or on some kind of mechanical appendage that pulls the wig along the double's abdomen and between her legs. Reduce labor costs and sanitation concerns, avoid lawsuits."

It doesn't take us 15 minutes to walk across town to a trendy restaurant, and already, right in front of us before the hostess's station, there's a young woman wearing a coat just like one of Carol's and with her hair given the same highlights and curls. "You've got five minutes to find out if she's a lesbian," my ridiculous friend says, as he withdraws back toward the doorway. "And if she is, is she as attracted to Rooney Mara as I am."

"And where are you going?"

"See if I can cadge a cigarette."

"I thought you quit five years ago."

"I did, but *Carol* made it all so glamorous again—hotel restaurants, fur coats and martinis, divorce, wealthy suburbs, chain smoking. I have to hold up the moviegoers' end of the bargain."

I can feel it coming on—one of Steven's speeches about product integration and George W.S. Trow. "'Entertainment' is an unsatisfactory word for what it"—the entertainment industry—"makes possible."

"Everybody drank and smoked back then," I note, leaving the woman with Cate Blanchett's hair and following Steve out onto the sidewalk. "Everybody drinks and smokes now, just different things. Now you're progressive if you fill your lungs with cannabis smoke and backward if it's nicotine."

"Yes, and half a century ago our wonderful *Carol* would have been a B movie about an evil lesbian sexual predator, and now—if only it had been Carol's husband using his wealth and age to pick up a struggling shop girl and take her to a series of motels—it could have been a Grade A movie about an evil male, heterosexual predator."

"So then the bottom line," I say, and this while noticing that the blonded woman is also coming out onto the sidewalk, "the bottom line is: nothing changes. The cars were too big then, they're too big now. Liquor and cigarette companies used to pay Hollywood to make drinking and smoking look glamorous, and now liquor and cigarette companies pay Hollywood to make drinking and smoking look glamorous."

He's smiling and only in part because he's gotten me to agree with him. Sensing an audience or hungry for this particular one, he raises his voice. "They even got into the *Carol* script a few lines about how great smoking was and how only stodgy, puritanical people objected to it. I wonder how much the industry paid to have Cate Blanchett say on screen: 'Just when you think things couldn't get any worse, you run out of cigarettes'?"

"What a bunch of cynics," the woman—less Hollywood than *Big Bang Theory*—butts in. "You want to put down a movie because the stars play lesbians—no interest in men, even successful ones."

She extracts from her purse a pack of American Spirit cigarettes ("organic tobacco and no additives does not mean a safer cigarette"). She offers us each one. "You missed the whole point of the movie. Do you realize what they were up against back then? Because of who she was—naturally—Carol loses her child. She's judged unfit as a mother. When Patricia Highsmith wrote the story—*her own story*—she had to publish it under a pseudonym. Now it's a 'major motion picture.' You have to admit that's incredible progress."

"What about the gun?" Steve says.

I have to admit it seemed a little odd—that for a cross-country road trip with Therese, Carol put a gun in her suitcase.

"How do you think that gun got there?" Steve presses.

"You tell me," the woman says. "A stagehand put it there?"

I lean toward her. "He's going to tell you the NRA paid a fee or that it was in Blanchett's contract—'I get to hold a gun.' Do you think it could be some lesbian thing?"

"Don't be silly, Ken," Steve butts in, and just when I'm trying to do some information gathering for him. "You just saw the movie. Figure it out. They're driving across country, stopping in motel after motel, and not having sex. One of the characters is a photographer. Neither is a conversationalist."

"So?" the woman and I both say (nice smiles at one another afterward).

"So," Steve, with his particular brand of self-confidence, says, "of course I'm not an 'insider,' but it went something like this. They screened the first cut for the backers, the money men, and during Carol and Therese's road trip one or more of the money men fell asleep or walked out of the room to go to take a piss with his cell-phone. What were 'they'—the producer, the director, Mara's people, Blanchett's people—gonna do? Cut the road trip, have Cate go down on Rooney in the very first motel they come to, or . . . ?

"Or?"

"You gotta know that producers have another file: scriptwriters who know how to juice up a movie at the last minute and without too much fuss or expense. Someone was called in. He or she came up with the gun idea. It just meant filming one new scene for the discovery of the gun and re-filming the discovery of the tape-recording scene so that the gun could be fired. Of course Blanchett couldn't actually shoot anyone. She couldn't hit the private detective even though he was just a few feet away. Never mind that this might or might not have been out of character—if she actually wings a human being, the whole last half hour of the movie would have to be re-shot.

"The big debate was: Should there be 'real' bullets in the gun, and she simply misses? Or should she have neglected to put bullets in the gun? Or even better, had it not occurred to her that guns take bullets? You have to admit it was a win-win, the entire movie was a win-win. Here's Blanchett, the big-shouldered dame made up like a drag queen and with voice and clothes like Lauren Bacall, and she's also that everlasting staple of vaudeville, Broadway and Hollywood: the dumb broad. Too stupid to know how to shoot a gun or to put bullets in it."

"The bottom line, if you ask me," the young woman says, "is

that you don't like movies. You missed the plot, the love affair, the battle with her husband for custody of their child."

"No, I saw all that," Steve says, "but so much more, too. You had a movie for lesbians and gays to come celebrate being able to be out of the closet after so many, very hard decades or centuries. And you had a movie for straight men who want nothing more than to have Rooney Mara and her double breasts whisper, 'Take me to bed.' You had a movie for the liquor, cigarette, and big-car companies, for the department stores, the cosmetics and perfume sellers, for Chicago's Drake Hotel. What did the Democrat Party used to call it—the Rainbow Coalition?"

The hostess and our new woman friend's woman friend are poking their heads out of the plastic, anti-winter-drafts doorway. Our tables are ready. And they are right next to one another. The hostess is ready and willing to push them together.

Now, finally, Steven is whispering. "I think the answer to my question may be no!"

He's talking about the young woman's sexual orientation. "So you're happy now," I say, skipping over another thing I've picked up: she's going to be sitting next to me.

But at least for the moment, he's calm—or, rather, grinning. "This is what I like most about American movies," he says. "Love always wins out in the end."

[11]
On Shunga and Learning How to Feel What When

The British Museum show *Shunga: Sex and Pleasure in Japanese Art* offered rooms of paintings and prints that were quite explicit without being particularly erotic. As at most every exhibit, the visitors passed slowly and quietly from one depiction (in this case, of Japanese people screwing) to the next depiction (of Japanese people screwing). The penises were enormous. One of the curators' best interventions was this quotation from a thirteenth-century writer: "The old masters . . . depict the size of 'the thing' far too large . . . If it were depicted the actual size there would be nothing of interest. For that reason, don't we say 'art is fantasy.'"

The lighting was dim, presumably to preserve the art works, which were produced in Japan between 1600 and 1900 (and then banned for much of the twentieth century). Visitors to the museum galleries had to concentrate yet more than usual in order to see something. Internally, privately, they may have been struggling, too, to figure out what they were supposed to see—what is essential in this show of representations of Japanese people having sex? The sex organs, the positions, the undergarments, facial expressions, colors, artistic techniques, the curators' descriptions of the works? Viewers' eyes shifted and lingered depending on their artistic and sexual tastes, and on their comfort/discomfort in looking at people having sex and in possibly being seen looking at images of people having sex.

I can see the possibilities for a comic sketch, in which museumgoers, moving slowly, studiously, from fuck to fuck, would be figures of fun. And the sketch, of course, would also have its socially redeeming side: helping us to think about our relation to art more generally—be the subject Balthus's guitar student with her dress around her ribs and her teacher's hand between her legs, or, say, Napoleon on his horse.

After wandering amid the obscurity and explicitness of the Shunga show, I sat down on a bench in the middle of one of the rooms. I had the idea that we, the viewers, were what was essential, the part of the show most worth paying attention to. But the twenty-first-century museumgoers' faces that I studied were not forthcoming or enlightening, except in their impassivity. I waited in vain to hear a little nervous laughter or a "Come see this!" I would have hardly been against a nice story whispered between fellow museumgoers, a story about the time when, after a nice glass of wine or on vacation in Japan, . . . Someone might have whispered something about what "we" might do that afternoon, back at our hotel. But no one did.

The curators' explications said that, among other uses, satire included, Shunga paintings and prints were given to young Japanese women when they were about to get married. The images were a kind of marriage manual, to show young brides how to behave, or handle themselves, in bed with a man. And without being too shocked by the actual size of their husbands' penises.

Or was it that the young bride was being pushed to see her husband's penis as larger—two or three times larger—than it actually was? Or was she being pushed yet further toward learning that, both in her bed and in her life, the ideal, the fantasy, was supposed to take the place of reality? And this even in her interactions with other women, however intimate or cold these might be. (We are approaching a basic role of art and of museums: the presentation—*voire* imposition or selling—of ideals.)

I am making my way toward an essence, presumably not the only essence, of this show. Clearly the Japanese women of that foreign age, like their young male partners and like youths in our times as well, were anxious to know not only what was going to happen in bed, in sex, but also what positions they were supposed to assume and—above all—what feelings they were supposed to express and to feel as well. A masculine desire to dominate, possess, penetrate? A feminine desire to be desired and "taken" by the male? Ecstasy, turmoil, hunger, aggression, tenderness, love? The fear of the rabbit or the pitiful pleas of a captive, naked before a soldier?

The deepening sorrow of the soldier or hunter, knowing that his gun cannot bring him closer to the being so present in his sight? Or is the requirement a series of feelings, felt or feigned and growing in strength or weakness, rising to some heavenly height or seeming increasingly instinctual and uncontrollable?

Such questions came to me after seeing a particular show concerning pre-modern Japan. Pictures, say, of twenty-first-century Londoners having sex would generate a somewhat different set of questions. (A joke of the British comedian Michael Flanders: "Always be sincere whether you mean it or not.")

In the present piece my interest is less in sincerity, or in what the possible feelings are, than in the fact that they are pre-established (e.g. by art and education of various sorts). And lovemakers young and old are at some pains to know what these feelings are. What is possible? Necessary? Acceptable? Inacceptable and therefore particularly erotic? Or considered disgusting or unimaginable.

It might not take all that long for any of us, to include a young, seventeenth-century Japanese woman, to appreciate that, in making love, we are supposed to seem to feel certain specific things, but this only leads us to the next task: How to show our partners, and by what means, that these requisite feelings are indeed what we are feeling in the midst of this sometimes complex dance, sometimes instinctual animal act? And it's not only our partners who need convincing; we, too, may wish to be convinced that we are feeling the requisite things. For young men how difficult can this be? If at the moment of ecstasy stuff comes out at the tip—success, mission accomplished, correct feelings felt and expressed. But for women, . . . To quote a female singer's pop hit (with the parenthetical asides in the original):

> How will I know? (Don't trust your feelings)
>
> How will I know? (Love can be deceiving)

In bed, more or less horizontal, and somehow both coupled and alone, the question may be rather: "Is this it?" Could there or should there be more, or less? Is this the effect he wants to have on me, and is this what it is supposed to, or not supposed, to be like or look like?

I would stress that the preceding paragraph has oversimplified the matter. Young men, for example, certainly have some of these worries that I have put on young women, and both sexes, or genders, are confronted with at times delicious, at times uneasy wondering about whether what "I" am feeling is much like what s/he is feeling? And all this may only appear to be simpler in homosexual couplings. And Freud has helped us recognize the further question: Is what "I" feel like I'm feeling much like what I am "really" feeling? To which a Wittgensteinian can add: What is this "really feeling"? Is it not precisely—or not precisely at all—the expressions that appear on "my" face or that, seemingly, like a protest, recriminations, flow from the skin of a burned finger to my brain? These feelings, be they expressed to others or within myself, are expressed in language, the structures and customs of which play a larger role in what "I" can express—or feel—than do any occasional impulses and circumstances. And so I might ask again, in vain, what am I really feeling, what was I really feeling when we made love? (And when I burn my finger, why, since such a network of nerves and brain cells are apparently involved in the unpleasant feeling, can I only feel it there—on the tip of my finger?)

THE WEEK AFTER seeing "Shunga: sex and pleasure in Japanese art," I went to see Hélène Cixous's play *L'histoire terrible mais inachevée de Norodom Sihanouk, roi du Cambodge*, a play about the man who remained the nominal, symbolic King of Cambodia after Pol Pot and the Khmer Rouge took over the country. At one point Cixous's protagonist says plaintively, « Je ne veux plus grimacer des sourires. » I want to stop grimacing smiles. How I (an American) would love to hear an American young woman say such a thing! Admit to such feelings. I take my 10-year-old son to have his photo taken in his soccer uniform—a fund-raising activity of the soccer league in which he plays and for which I coach. The photographer has my son hold a ball under his right arm, put his right foot on a box and "smile," which is to say: show as much of as many teeth as possible, the upper row in particular. What do the feelings being staged and recorded on this occasion have to do with soccer or my son? What do they have to do with this boy at this moment posing as part of his Dad paying for a photo as a way of contributing money to pay for uniforms, use of field, etc.? In a sense these questions are irrelevant. What is relevant is that Jonah has to smile. Without a smile the photographer may be upbraided and downgraded by his boss. And if Jonah can smile—and in the face of his father's ranting against the system, against forced-feigned emotions—is Jonah, at least, happy?

We may note that for museum visitors, too, there are also required feelings—feelings that it needs to seem like you, the visitor, are feeling. Inside the museum's marble walls, at the Shunga exhibit, it seemed that, above all, the feeling required, of men and women, was impassivity. There may well have been a little intellectual-visual something passing between the erotic drawings behind glass and brain cells in back of viewers' eyes. But as for their own cocks or cunts—why do you feel it necessary to use such words?

[12]
Distancing / Awareness

Originally delivered as a speech to a conference of the Association of Graduate Liberal Studies Programs. Revised for print publication.

The Personal, The Political, and The Intellectual

Zeteo, the on-line journal I edit, takes a particular interest in articles and essays that combine personal, political, and intellectual perspectives. On a simple level this means that we urge writers to include in their pieces discussion of how they have come to their subjects, and to not be afraid of using autobiographical examples or of expressing political views. We have an idea that the result is a more "holistic" and more truthful work, because the writer's particular perspective and interests are part of the discussion rather than being denied and kept under wraps.

This approach also makes a philosophical claim. This claim certainly connects with Nietzsche's idea that there are no facts, only interpretations. But I would put the matter another way: if writers and readers include in their discussions information or ruminations about their particular perspectives and about the sources of their work, the understanding on offer will be broader and deeper. Further, the work will speak to what human knowledge may be and to its limitations.

In speaking of the "sources" of a given piece, what do I have in mind? One answer would have to do with how the research, the writing time, and the writer were paid for. Another answer would focus on techniques—first-hand research or secondary texts, empiricism or induction, etc. Another answer speaks to the writer's motivations for doing the work. Why, for example, did Vanessa Badagliacca, a *Zeteo* contributor, decide to devote a not insignificant portion of her life to writing about a Chinese artist's environmental sculpture, *Doing Nothing Garden*, and about how it connects to Arte

Povera and to writings of Gilles Clément and Giorgio Agamben?

Badagliacca addresses this question in several places in the piece, to include in the introduction. This from the beginning:

> I grew up hearing the recurring expression that if you . . . didn't catch "the train" passing right at that moment you would miss it. You would lose your chance to do something, to meet someone, to experience something, to get something, to take the chance of a lifetime. Reflecting on Song Dong's *Doing Nothing Garden*, I am more and more convinced that "doing nothing" is not only an active attitude, but even a dynamic attitude. . . . "Doing nothing" is not the opposite of "doing." Recognizing the dual existence of these two concepts may help us regain our balance.

This is also to say that the work was helping Badagliacca regain her own balance.

Where We're Going from Here

The rest of this piece will focus on Jean-Luc Godard's movie *Sympathy for the Devil* (or *1 + 1*) and Alfred Kinsey's reports on human, or mid-twentieth-century American, sexuality. Albeit haltingly, these works point the way toward some of the larger advantages and also challenges of more holistic—or more "self-conscious"—work.

To head off confusion I need to stress that the Godard example broadens the discussion, leading it beyond questions of motivation. The Kinsey example will run us smack into the intersection of the personal, political, and intellectual, and point up how difficult such holistic work can be. In this way I am underscoring another aspect of the *Zeteo* project: exploration, to include the questioning our own assumptions. "Zeteo" is an ancient Greek and New Testament word which has been translated as to challenge, to question, to seek honestly, to dispute, to debate and pose alternative ideas and solutions. I hope that this is indeed what the journal and the present text involve.

Sympathy for the Devil

Sympathy for the Devil found a home in this paper, and indeed this whole paper took shape, thanks to a line in the British film theorist Laura Mulvey's seminal article on the male gaze: "Visual Pleasure and Narrative Cinema" (*Screen 3*, Autumn 1975). At one point Mulvey writes about how commercial films "eliminate intrusive camera presence and *prevent* a distancing awareness in the audience" (my italics). With the word "distancing," she is noting that filmmakers do not want to interfere with the viewers' suspension of disbelief, their absorption in the movie, and their voyeuristic pleasure. In this context "awareness" is a problem; it gets in the way. I would linger here a moment because we often think of "distancing" and "awareness" as being at opposite ends of a spectrum, and because the present paper seeks to make a case for less distancing and more integration, and therefore for more awareness.

Personally, I often find that when I go to the movies something like the camera in fact does intrude at certain moments: during nude scenes and sex scenes. When, in a darkened movie theater, I see, say, a young woman leaving her boyfriend on the rocks as she strips off her clothes and dives naked into a mountain pool, I often find myself wondering about and indeed picturing the director in his chair, and various technicians with their booms and lenses surrounding the actors, and the miles of cables, the sandwiches and coffee laid out on side tables. It seems to me that at such moments I am having a fuller experience of the movie than when I am more distanced from the production process. It is not that I am "seeing more" of an actor's flesh; I am seeing the illusion more clearly and understanding it better. I would be seeing even more were I at the same time able to hear the various negotiations about the script and lighting. I would like, too, to overhear the negotiations involving money. The movie and this scene are, after all, first and foremost a commercial product. Views of scantily clothed, youthful, and physically attractive women and men have been a staple of the entertainment business for many, many years, and so there is a sense in which a woman's naked dive into a pond is only secondarily a "plot element." Viewers are being offered a strip tease, and by starting from this fact we could come to understand the scene more fully than if, with distanced awareness, we focused on the motivations of the character the naked actress is ostensibly bringing to celluloid or pixelated life.

There is a sense in which the whole point of this paper is right here. To offer another, more academic example, imagine an article on the social spiders of Brazil that allowed its readers at key moments to see elements of a larger picture—the incredible agricultural productivity that has freed some humans to devote their lives to doing studies that seem to have no direct economic or political value; the psychological motivations that may drive an individual to study social spiders; the challenges of human solitude and sociability that may serve as a backdrop. By not touching on such things—by using the rhetoric of "objective" scholarship to keep readers (and, indeed, the author too) distanced from this larger picture or pictures—the writers prevent "a distancing awareness" in their audience. By narrowing our vision, they may increase our escapist pleasure, the escapist pleasure of empirical scientific research, I am calling this. In *les Pensées* Pascal points out that human beings can be diverted—from the truth and the divine—not only by cue sticks and billiard balls, but also by mathematics problems and by analyzing human behavior, and by the pursuit of intellectual celebrity.

Sympathy for the Devil (1968) is one movie in which a filmmaker experiments with allowing viewers to see more of the filmmaking process. It is a frustrating movie to watch (and I am ready to send my DVD off to anyone interested). The movie is frustrating not least because half of it offers us a behind the scenes look at the Rolling Stones recording one of their hits, but this "look"—take after take of the same song—keeps making us feel that we do not understand how the song was created or how it was made into a hit. During the same period, a French satirical song about the media had the refrain "Plus on apprend plus on ne sait rien." (The more we learn, the less we know.) I take this to be a theme of Godard's movie as well. We are awash in media, information, and claims of meaning, and these are like an ever-expanding wall between us and understanding. And, yes, this is one of the questions this paper is asking: do articles and essays that combine the personal, the political, and the intellectual widen our understanding and thus, inter alia, further swamp us and/or push us to recognize the frustrating limits of human understanding? Can such writing help us appreciate how we are confined (or held securely?) by our subjectivity, by our view through one particular lens, or through a particular set of lenses: the human set?

In my favorite *Sympathy for the Devil* scene, "Eve Democracy," an attractive young woman in a white frock, is wandering barefoot in a scruffy, over-exposed forest. Swirling around her is a meager film crew, which is engaged in a charade, since the film we are watching cannot be their work, since we see them in it. An interviewer peppers Eve with questions: "Do you feel exploited . . . the moment you step into an interview?" "Orgasm is the only moment when you can't cheat life?" One has a feeling that the director has allowed the actress to answer as she wishes, but with only these two words: "Yes" or "No." She enjoys complete freedom to be meaningless?

Sympathy for the Devil was hardly a great commercial success, and its interest in presenting, simultaneously, distancing fantasies and some of the means of their production certainly played a role in limiting its receipts. My sense is that it is much the same with "holistic" intellectual articles, essays, and books. If the writer is willing and able to speak to us about why and how the work was produced, he, or she, may heighten our understanding and thus in some senses deny us pleasures, diversions from the truth and the divine. The writer may induce "distancing awareness," denying us the safe refuge we often seek in intellectual work, pushing us to see what we would not.

Of course this desire to limit our view is not only psychological. I recall a heart specialist's observation that for a period of ten years or so it was impossible to get funding for or to publish research that challenged the efficacy of statin drugs, which had become a multibillion-dollar business, a business fueled in part by the all-too-human wish to believe that science can indeed come up with miracle cures, erasing the human predicament, our mortality included. This is not to say that during this period earnest people did not do earnest experiments with statins, doing their best to produce objective evidence, reproducible results. But the camera was never pulled back to show the context in which the research was being done, a context in which certain questions could not be asked and in which funds and jobs were available, and only available, to those interested in exploring certain other questions. (I am reminded of the iconoclastic painter Robert Cenedella's observation about museums and art galleries: "It's not what they show, it's what they don't show.")

It is easy enough these days to meet or read about scientists who shifted the focus of their research to subjects that were attracting more funding and whose devotees were winning more of the prizes. And if we are to say that the pool-diving scene was fundamentally about the ongoing economic viability of striptease, we might say, too, that a good deal of scientific research is about the pursuit of funding and prizes, or, more simply, ambition. (This was the theme of a book that made a great impression on me when I was growing up—James Watson and Francis Crick's *The Double Helix*, about the race to discover the structure of DNA and, thereby, win a Nobel Prize.)

Kinsey and the Kinsey Reports

I will now offer the example of an intellectual work that, though controversial and groundbreaking, avoided taking up personal and political challenges that were central to its production. It will be seen that it would have been impossible for the principal author and his colleagues to have taken up these challenges, and yet, at the same time, I believe the example shows how much more might have been learned if this impossibility had not stood in the way. The work is Alfred Kinsey's (and the Institute for Sex Research at Indiana University's) *Sexual Behavior in the Human Male* and *Sexual Behavior in the Human Female*, also known as the Kinsey Reports.

The account on offer here owes a good deal to two excellent biographies: Jonathan Gathorne-Hardy, *Kinsey: Sex the Measure of All Things: A Life of Alfred C. Kinsey* (Indiana University Press, 1998) and James H. Jones, *Alfred C. Kinsey: A Public/Private Life* (W.W. Norton, 1997). From Jones's Preface and then much later on in his text:

> In recent years there has been a tendency to argue that if science is the produce of personal needs and motivations, then this somehow discredits scientific discoveries. Yet Kinsey's science was driven by needs that were not simply idiosyncratic but deeply embedded in our culture. His problems, albeit in exaggerated form, were the nation's problems.

> However much he [Kinsey] talked about science's need for data, this was not his primary motivation. Again, his research sprang from a private agenda shaped by personal politics. Decades of inner turmoil had transformed Kinsey into a rebel, a man who rejected the sexual mores of his age. He meant to change the public's thinking on sexual matters. Convinced that cold, hard facts alone would persuade the public to develop more tolerant sexual attitudes, Kinsey was determined to provide those data.

Prior to becoming a famous sex researcher, Kinsey had a successful academic career as an entomologist. His particular interest was the differences within species, and he studied this subject with a furious, *voire* sadistic, compulsivity, traveling the US and Mexico to collect, it is said, more than 5 million examples of gall wasps. As insect collectors are wont to do, he killed these individuals (5 million of them?) and pinned and labelled them, and he measured more than twenty different aspects of their anatomies, along the way demonstrating that there were substantial, significant differences between individuals of this species. Subsequently, more famously and much more influentially, he used a similarly compulsive approach to gathering data about human sexuality and made a similar argument that there were substantial, significant variations in our sexual inclinations and behaviors, and that these variations were as normal as those of the wasps.

Insofar as we have an eye out for the role of money, we would like to explore, too, the motivations of those in and around Indiana University and the Rockefeller Foundation: the supporters of Kinsey's sex research. (They supported his work to advance their own various interests, to include in de-stigmatizing homosexuality and in developing social policies and programs to better control human sexual behavior.) I would also not ignore the no-facts-only-interpretations perspective with which this piece began. And yet, this said, I will now focus on the currently dominant interpretation of how the personal, political, and intellectual combined in Kinsey's own research and writing.

Since Kinsey's death, in 1956, it has come out that he had a powerful personal interest in the conclusions he reached. He himself was by nature quite promiscuous and had strong homosexual and masochistic urges that were not considered normal or acceptable in the society in which he grew up. For most of his lifetime, and even after the publication of his research, these variations (to include urethral insertions and tying a rope around his scrotum and tugging hard while he masturbated) were not considered part of the normal range of variations acceptable in the human species (or in Americans at least). Rather, the variations were considered frighteningly abnormal.

Supposing that Kinsey, just for his part, had been more upfront about the personal and political purposes of his research. (With "political" here being used not to refer to elections, but to social attitudes and roles more generally.) Let's not skip over the first challenge: such upfrontness or transparency might have demanded a degree of self-examination of which Kinsey was not capable, and understandably so. (He was a human being.) The biographical materials I have read have given me the impression that it was only through doing his research that Kinsey got in touch with the extent of his homosexual and masochistic urges. It was his research that took him to what could now be called "gay" bars in Chicago, and it was patrons of these bars who realized better than Kinsey himself that he was not just there to get more of his surveys filled out.

Secondarily, there is the obvious fact that if Kinsey had been able to be upfront about the personal interests and "political" goals he brought to the research, the entire research project and its conclusions would have been called into question, and likely the research would never have been completed and Kinsey's impact on American society would have been minimal at best. The funding would have dried up and any preliminary conclusions, no matter how accurate or applicable to or useful for many more people than Kinsey and his backers, would not have been taken seriously. (My sense is that these "facts," about the rules that govern the theater of modern science, are yet more significant than those that Kinsey uncovered or proposed as regards human sexuality.)

The calling into question of Kinsey's work would have been two pronged. On the one hand it would have been insisted, well before the research was done, that, first and foremost, sexual promiscuity and homosexual urges and behavior were sinful or perverse and hardly as prevalent as Kinsey's surveys suggested they were. On the other hand it would have been argued that given the lead researcher's sexual proclivities and political interests—that is, given his interest in having his and many others' proclivities gain greater public acceptance and not seem perverse—the research could not be objective.

I do not want to divert this paper into a discussion of the possibility or impossibility of scholarly objectivity. I think the simplest approach then is simply to put my cards on the table, to say that this paper has been written with the presumption that scholarly objectivity is an illusion that, among other things, "prevents a distancing awareness in the audience." That is, the putative objectivity allows readers to get lost in the subject much as viewers happily lose themselves in a darkened movie theater. They lose track of the extent to which Eve Democracy—or, say, Eve Entomologist or Eve Theoretical Physicist—is performing, following a script, speaking to the desires and fears of her audience, as well as to her own.

By Way of Conclusion

Watching *Sympathy for the Devil* viewers could feel annoyed, wishing and not being fully able to enter into a false, voyeuristic intimacy with the music industry or with Eve Democracy (the character, or with Anne Wiazemsky, the actress). But these viewers would also find themselves, perhaps against their wills, in greater touch with the nature and business of voyeurism. More "holistic" statin research might have given us less information—however questionable—about statins, and yet in telling us more about the terms under which medical research is done, it would have given us yet more valuable insight into the Lipitor, Crestor, et al., that our doctors keep urging upon us and also into the whole world of pharmacology in which we and our health and our finances are caught up, and the world of faith to which we turn when the terms of our existence seem unbearable.

The wave of sexual liberation that crested around 1970 has receded. The pressures of church, community, and family values on individuals' sexual lives have been more than replaced by the pressures of employers, peers, and conformism, and by the uses of sex to sell products and services on television and everywhere else. Should we say that sex requires not just private spaces but space in the mind and uncluttered, un-impinged-upon time, time when one is content to be doing nothing but what one is doing and to be in contact with no one but the person one may be having sex with. And such space and time has been largely given and taken away.

Nonetheless, for a brief, wonderful moment, the Kinsey reports did help liberate the sex lives of many Americans—gay, straight, and otherwise. From Jones:

> Of course, Kinsey's work did not cause the shifts in sexual attitudes and behavior that occurred in the United States during his lifetime. First, those shifts had been under way for several decades before his books were published, as Kinsey himself documented so richly; and second, they were driven more by social and economic changes than by the work of sex researchers. What Kinsey did accomplish was to bring intimate matters into the open so that people could discuss them with unprecedented candor. This cultural dialogue, in turn, helped shape what followed.

I consider Kinsey a great American and believe his biography helps us understand the sources and motivations of a great deal of our science. But I am also here to say that a more honest, more transparent approach could have led to a yet richer, fuller, and more informative result than the startling results that were achieved. Among other things, such a project could have spoken to the interconnections between research and funding and personal and political agendas. It could have given us "facts" that were not distanced or disconnected from the context in which they were created, the ongoing dialogue in which they intervened. It might have spoken more deeply about human knowledge, and how it always has self-interested and political components.

[13]
Professional Primates

IN THE CAFÉ CAR OF AN AMTRAK TRAIN, a businesswoman in her fifties asked if she might sit across from me. It was a Friday evening. She, a senior manager at a Boston biotech company, was on her way to meet her husband and teenage children, who seemed to be, thanks to her high salary, enjoying life on a boat. Across from me she immediately opened her MacBook. She had to create slides for a presentation the next week.

On a napkin I scribbled a "Haiku to Businesswoman on the 5.35":

> the light from your Mac
>
>   is washing the color out
>
> of a lovely face

I did not show her my poem, but there may have been something in my occasional glances. She took out her compact and re-did her lips, and then, using the window as a mirror, ran her fingers through her expensively colored hair, trying to give it a little more life.

A few days later I read a *Current Biology* report in which scientists were describing the mating patterns of chimpanzees in a Ugandan national park. Male chimps, the authors proposed, prefer to mate with females who are 30 years of age or older. These older females are also more often fought over by males. Apparently, even balding 55-year-old females with worn and broken teeth are more appealing to males than are young healthy females. The authors proposed that the appeal of older females may be that they have been successful, both in surviving and in reproducing, in having and raising children. (A reminder of how science mirrors social trends, and of how social trends are rooted in economics. Now that we have a growing population of aging female humans with plenty of their own money and holding managerial jobs, we are finding that, even in the wild, even among chimpanzees, aging females are attractive.)

Meanwhile, in the café car, the businesswoman and I got into a good conversation about the differential abilities and performance of boys and girls at school and of men and women in organizations. Normally I would have proposed that she and I exchange business cards, continue our conversation on some other occasion. Although it is highly unlikely we would have had sex, we were well on our way to having the thought cross one or both of our minds.

But she was eager to meet her family for dinner and get on the boat, and I wanted to get to my New York apartment, my teenage son, my own bed, and sleep. And my goals were being well met until, back home, around midnight, the college kids and med students once again began congregating in the park-like space surrounding my apartment building. Emboldened by alcohol, short skirts, breast flesh, the males were roaring, and the females, in their turn were crying out—attracting and fending off male advances. It was a while before security staff bothered to disperse the roving bands, and then I still had to fall back asleep. In the early morning hours, I heard the tender, animal sounds of a young female—perhaps on her back, buttocks red, labia swollen—on one of the cement chess tables below.

LATER THAT WEEKEND I went to a meeting of a scholarly professional association. It was held in the apartment of one of the board members. I rode my bike there—six or seven miles. When I arrived—flushed from the exercise and with my backpack—the hostess said it looked like I had been hiking. Through the jungle, I might now say.

The association is open to both men and women and might attract equal numbers of both sexes. But associating—or at least meeting to plan future meetings and to discuss communication strategies—may increasingly be a women's thing. And this particular meeting was being held on a fall Sunday afternoon—that is, on a football Sunday afternoon. About a dozen women attended, but, apart from me there was only one other man, and he a jovial, soft-fleshed man, neutered by the fact that his chosen profession had been decimated by the Internet.

I quickly took my place in the living room, next to an attractive young woman. She was one of the few woman there who was still of childbearing age (or of what used to be called childbearing age). It is also the case that, because of how attractive I found her looks and demeanor, over the past year I had found various excuses for corresponding with this young woman by e-mail. But I had never felt it was quite appropriate, or that her interest was sufficient, for me to suggest a coffee. And for all I know she lives with a partner, be this person a man or a woman. And so what interested me then was how, when—with the Giants game about to start—I excused myself from the meeting, this young woman came to the vestibule to say good-bye to me, and in private.

May a reader of *Current Biology* reports be excused for proposing that when a viral male comes through the jungle to where females are gathered, it is for coitus. And a young fertile female understands this and presents to the male, and this even if, when the time comes, she is going to say she's too busy for coffee or, later, that the man has misunderstood, she wasn't interested in *that kind* of relationship. (Or in that kind of coitus.)

I was surprised and delighted that Ingrid, I will call her, came to say good-bye, but there was another aspect of my socio-sexual response at the meeting that surprised me more. During the meeting we were sitting in a circle, Ingrid on my left and across from me a middle-aged woman, closer to my age, already the mother of teenagers. Though their womanliness, their vitality was muted by her simple, comfortable clothing, the woman's breasts were ample, her hips wide. Naked, Elizabeth (let's call her) could have been a model for a fertility god. (That is, she had physical features that have long been associated with female fertility and nurture.)

What surprised me—what led to this piece—was that there seemed to be something in the social structure of this meeting, or in human beings' changing social relations more generally, that led my eyes to be drawn to this woman, Elizabeth, and that led me to think about her afterwards, and not in scholarly or professional ways. Yes, I never saw and have not cared to see the Amtraking senior manager's slide presentation, and I am here ignoring the intellectual talents and interests of the associating women and what they and I said about the scholarly projects we were working on—projects in anthropology, ethics, musicology, the psychology of art—projects that quite interest another side of me. A Freudian might speak here of sublimation, of how some of us (and even I, with a disconcerting regularity) rise above our animal instincts, using our libidinal energy for higher purposes. This would be to ignore how often such "sublimation" is not so much a rising above as escape and denial, a pretending to be other than we really are.

Yes, in addition to libidos and other instinctual drives, our species has some intellectual capacities. And these may, for example, allow us to observe, reflect on, and write about our instinctual and emotional responses. And, as I have written elsewhere, even these seemingly intellectual observations are themselves instinctual and emotional responses, and hardly less so because they are couched in language that seeks to hide or deny their true sources.

The night after that Sunday meeting, lying in bed, waiting on sleep, my thoughts came back to Elizabeth and my attraction to her, and then—unable to hold on to these thoughts or to do anything with half-remembered images—I slipped away into wondering about my seeming change of heart, of desire. I had always thought I was drawn to the slim-hipped and small-breasted, to a girlish demeanor (no matter the woman's actual age). Yet now there was Elizabeth and the businesswoman on the train. Was it my newfound motherlessnees, my aged mother having recently died? Was it economics? Women have long found older men who appear to have money or power to be particularly handsome, and even to like "rugged good looks" that seem downright ugly in lower-status men. Perhaps my eyesight had been now similarly reprogrammed; female money, status, and professional competence were looking good to me, sexy.

I recalled reading about other mammalian species in which the females kept together and the males wandered far, each by himself, a male only sneaking or striding (or bicycling) back when he smelled the females in heat or when he himself felt the urge to copulate or reproduce. A female might move to the edge of the group, where she could be most easily smelled or seen, separated from the rest, briefly taken by a lone wolf (or lone primate). In other locales—on the sidewalks of my youthful neighborhood, for example—one may also see queen females surrounded by several ladies in waiting. Alpha males have to push these others out of the way to get to the women they want, the women who, in a sense, are reserving themselves for the most successfully pushy.

I found myself reminded, too, of a real-estate transaction in which I had recently been involved. The real estate was, at least in some legal sense, mine, but the transaction was overseen by a host of women who had another idea. They would arrange everything and then I would sign. (Sperm become ink? And instead of trying to ejaculate in the vaginas of the attractive young woman and the fertility god of the professional association, I write about them?)

ON THE WEB I have found a description of the various structures of primate societies, including "polygynous families" (a.k.a. the "one-male-several-female group"):

> Mothers, sisters, and aunts act as a team in chasing off other unrelated females. They also collectively select their mutual mate among a number of potential suitors roaming in and out of their territory. The male that is chosen usually is one that does not act abusively towards them and is willing to cooperate with them in defending their territory. The relationship with any particular male may be short-term. The stable core of the community is the group of related females.

Not only the moral messages of our science, but also the social structures of we human primates seem to be rapidly evolving. Is the male-female partner-pairs model of the past several hundred years giving way to associations of women and lone males? I can imagine women losing interest in men, except insofar as some males may need to be encouraged to make deposits at sperm banks or to help in the fabrication and distribution of vibrators and other sex toys. In a less extreme model, viral males will occasionally seek to raid the female associations and to try to carry off (or seduce away) one or more of the fertile females. These women may have brief careers of ecstasy and pain before returning back to the group, tails and tales between their legs. In a beehive, the female worker bees shift roles as they age, at times nurturing, manufacturing, or guarding, at times taking out the dead bodies or going in search of nectar. Similarly, in my vision, once promiscuous human females shift to being mothers, lawyers, teachers, nurses, businesswomen, and police—all the various roles needed by the group.

By the winds of capitalism and of less-human elements, we are swept along and through vast changes, driven here and there by forces much more powerful than any one of us and than all of us put together. And yet, being human, we persist in imagining we are making significant choices, that each healthy adult is capable of making significant choices. I may choose Ingrid or Elizabeth, and Ingrid, Elizabeth, or Sarah may choose me or choose to reject me. We amuse and soothe ourselves with our fantasies as a train rumbles down tracks that we ourselves have constructed with our own cleverness and sweat, and without knowing—usually without even thinking about—where we may really be headed, what ends we may in fact be serving.

"Oh, the places you'll go!" Dr. Seuss once put it, optimistically. And I am reminded, too, of his Lorax, who spoke for the trees, as the Once-ler, with a surging enthusiasm and desperation, was destroying the entire forest, in order to make more and more Thneeds, "which everyone needs". Oh the places we are going. And yet, even in our trains, our "monkey suits," our meetings, parks, bedrooms, intellectual essays—it's ever a jungle.

[IV]
Politics

Man . . . has a strong propensity to isolate himself from others, because he finds in himself at the same time the unsocial characteristic of wishing to have everything go his way. Meanwhile he expects opposition on all sides because, in knowing himself, he knows that he, for his own part, is inclined to oppose others. This opposition awakens all his powers, brings him to conquer his inclination to laziness, and, propelled by vainglory, lust for power, and avarice, to achieve a rank among his fellows, whom he can neither endure nor do without.

> — Immanuel Kant, *Idee zu einer allgemeinen Geschichte in weltbürgerlicher Absicht* (Idea for a Universal History from a Cosmopolitan Point of View), using translation by Lewis White Beck

[14]

The American Flag is at Half-Mast Today

The American flag is at half-mast today because the person whose job it is to pull the thing all the way up, and who indeed sometimes does—unfortunately he got a call on his phone right when he was in the middle of doing his job. We can't tell you how sorry we are about that.

The American flag is at half-mast today because I—and frankly I don't know why they always expect me to do this job—but I had a dental appointment or one of my kids was sick or I just made an honest mistake, what's so bad about that? So maybe I thought it was a holiday when it wasn't. And, in any case, I sent an e-mail before noon, or maybe just a little bit after. I assumed that John, who's such a nice man, would pull the flag up, as he usually does when I am not able to get in right away. But obviously something went wrong, probably with the network—something is always going wrong with the network, don't you think? It's too bad, about the network and also about the flag.

I can personally assure you that the flag is not at half-mast today and that it has always been company policy to raise the flag to the very top of the mast except on those days when we receive official notification that an important person has died, which, our records will show clearly, we have not received in this case.

It is a sad day when, for whatever reason, the American flag does not make it all the way to the very top, where it of course belongs, and let me first assure all of you that my administration will do everything in its power to find out who among our internal enemies, who do not appreciate all that this country has done for them, or among our many external enemies, who will stop at nothing to oppose the imposition of American freedom and democracy on the rest of the world and to destroy our very way of life, our sources of oil and computer chips, and the many decent, law-abiding and hard-working consumers of our football and basketball T-shirts. And may I say further that, thanks to one of our great American traditions that has allowed our great presidents to ignore our great laws and our great constitution when they feel that great circumstances warrant such bold action, and thanks to our global hegemony and advanced military systems that allow us to kill, somewhat indiscriminately and certainly without bothering with so-called due process, which is not all it's cracked up to be—I can personally assure you that in this case, as in every case, evildoers will be identified and they will be killed, and a new department will be created and thousands if not millions of Americans will be given steadily low-paying jobs—not to actually pull up any flags, of course, but to ensure that—whether, whatever, or whenever our flags are pulled or not—from this day forward correct procedures will be correctly followed.

I DON'T KNOW WHY YOU THINK the American flag is at half-mast today. This is the height to which the flag has always been pulled, and we've never had anyone complain about it before. I'm sorry if you see things differently. We'd be glad to allow you to give it a double-pull if you'd like. All you need do is register on-line for this absolutely free service which will also entitle you to be among the first to hear about our other great products.

WE HAVE HEARD THAT THE AMERICAN FLAG is at half-mast today. In such circumstances, when it turns out that no one important has died and yet the flag, for whatever reason, has never gotten pulled all the way up—normally a correction would be issued, so that the record comes to show that the flag was indeed—or, if you prefer, should have been or indeed should be—at full mast. But given that tomorrow we expect the flag will be back up at the top, what we've decided is that this is a situation in which it is not appropriate to issue a correction or to take any further action regarding the flag's placement. It may well be that the puller-upper has had a good reason for making the decision she seems to have made, and in any case, it's just best, it's our policy; the senior management team has met to discuss this matter, and we have reviewed our decision with the Director, and again, making a correction, as if a mistake had been made—we have decided that this is not appropriate at the present time given our policies.

The American flag is at half-mast today because I, the God-forsaken puller-upper, yes, I was talking on the phone while working, and, yes, it was my cock-sucking wife on the other end who started telling me about how the car I just bought for her last week—and even though, yada-yada, didn't I remember how she had said she had her suspicions?—but no, the not unattractive saleswoman had told me the car been given the "100% Gold rating" under the new "No Regrets personalized inspection system®," and 100% ratings were extremely rare, and I was lucky to be able to get such a car at such a price, and now it needs a goddamn new transmission, and . . . Frankly, I'm sorry about the flag, but you can go fuck yourself and this whole fucking country. I don't know why I even bother to come to work, to earn money for what? So I end up with a "new used" car that needs a brand-new-fucking-used transmission for a fucking $1,999 plus tax, plus you can put right up your ass the new brakes and fuel-injection system it will also turn out to need before my credit card can go bust and I am allowed to move the thing from the garage to the junkyard and turn my plates in to your fucking Department of Motor Vehicles where—if you want to know my honest fucking opinion—the flag should always be at half-mast!

I understand that you are quite concerned about the fact that the American flag is at half-mast today, and even though, it seems, no one important has died, but this is a complex matter. I know you think it inappropriate that my campaign has received what you call "substantial" contributions from the Half-Mast Company and from the Sustainable Green Profit Agenda, which it may apparently have some involvement with. I have heard, too, as you apparently have, that this company has done some, perhaps not a lot, of outsourcing of flag raising to people who have the advantage of being born without arms and who are therefore happy to pull on flags as best they can for one dollar an hour and without health insurance, vacations, or weekends. And may I personally say that I think that, in the long run, it is not only better for the global economy, it is also better for our economy and indeed for you and me if our flag-raising is handled in the most cost-effective manner, and especially when you consider the number of flags that need raising and how the entrepreneurial genius of Half-Mast's founder and her venture capital backers have led the company to new market highs, and this even as the company has yet to turn a profit and there have been some glitches in its wonderful program to allow each star of the flag to memorialize an American killed by terrorists or friendly fire, while also advertising the products of one of our 50 greatest multinational corporations, the vast majority of whose profits are reported in small-island tax havens, but whose headquarters are right here in the United States of America!

THE AMERICAN FLAG IS AT HALF-MAST TODAY, but I am single woman and gluten is now giving me hives and also nuts, and I think I'm on the spectrum, and nobody realized this when I was growing up, and I just heard that my neighbor's son-in-law's mindfulness app got an orphan virus and she wants me to go visit him in the hospital.

WE ARE EXPERIENCING VERY HIGH CALL VOLUMES. If you would please spell your first name and last name and clearly state the account number that appears on the back of your bill, the last four digits of your Social Security number, your zip code, and your birthdate, we appreciate your patience, a representative will be right with you and will not be able to fully understand English or be able to help you with your problem, which, if you would please consult your contract, you will see it is not our responsibility, and at the end of this call it will be appreciated if you could take a short survey because customer service is very important to us.

[15]
Ditch the Term Pathogen

A SHORT COMMENT, published in the 11 December 2014 issue of *Nature* and entitled "Ditch the term pathogen," is the most interesting, thought-provoking piece that I have ever read in that distinguished science magazine, and, over the years, I have read quite a few. The argument of the authors, Arturo Casadevall and Liise-anne Pirofski, is that the idea that diseases are caused by external agents—pathogens, bad microbes—is incorrect and part of an oversimplistic paradigm.

This paradigm, which can be associated with "germ theory," has long been considered the triumph of "scientific medicine," which took hold in the nineteenth century thanks to the work of such great scientists as Louis Pasteur and Robert Koch, and of Claude Bernard (1813-78), the founder of experimental physiology. Because it helps frame the medical and political discussions of the present piece, I will here call particular attention to one of Bernard's best-known views: that the human body (and other living bodies), though it has need of its surrounding environment, is nevertheless relatively independent of it. Our tissues are separated from direct external influences and are protected from them (e.g. by our immune systems). Disease occurs when something bad enters our bodies from the outside and overwhelms our defenses.

With politics as well as medicine on my mind, I note that the pathogen or germ-theory paradigm may bring to mind George W. Bush and his (or his speechwriters') axis of evil. In this paradigm, as in many of our ideas about health and sanitation, "I" or "we" (the United States) are basically good and pure, and so the danger is that we may be invaded or infected by evil, corruption, disease outside ourselves. To remain healthy, we have to build up our defenses and also attack our enemies, weakening their power to do us harm. Thus, for example, we use drones to try to kill "terrorists" (anti-US, non-state actors) in foreign countries. And we believe that if our espionage and screening procedures can identify dangerous external agents and their weapons, and do away with them before they, say, get on our airplanes, we will at least be able to travel safely.

A different paradigm is offered by the FBI's COINTELPRO program and related FBI activities of the 1950s, 60s, and 70s. One of its techniques for combating Americans who were, for example, active in the Civil Rights and anti-Vietnam-War movements was to try to create and foster personal conflicts among activists and to arouse suspicions about their sexual and financial activities. As the human rights activist Aryeh Neier writes in a review of a book by former *Washington Post* reporter Betty Medsger, "the FBI sent 'poison pen' letters to break up marriages; there were incitements by the FBI to gang warfare; and members of a violent group were falsely [proclaimed to be] police informers." The relevant medical disease model is of bad things happening when the "normal flora" within the organism become deranged or get out of control. (Donald Trump gets elected.)

I note that this paradigm can apply whether you believe that Hoover was out of control or that, say, Martin Luther King Jr., the target of COINTELPRO's most sustained campaign, was out of control. It is also important to note, however, that Hoover himself was working with a germ-theory paradigm: King, white Leftists, and American Indians were all outsiders, external agents, trying to destroy some otherwise healthy inside of white America. The paradigm of the Civil Rights and anti-war activists was that the organism itself was corrupt, with this corruption certainly linked to the foundation of the republic as a democracy that condoned slavery.

CLEARLY I AM QUITE INTERESTED in political observations that Casadevall and Pirofski's note may inspire, but I am also interested in the purely medical perspective, and this, and not politics, is the entire focus of the *Nature* piece. Thus the scientists—professors at the Albert Einstein College of Medicine at Yeshiva University in New York—first recognize that the pathogen paradigm has been associated with some of medicine's great successes, for example the development of vaccines for tetanus and diphtheria. But, they write:

> the use of the term pathogen sustains an unhelpful focus among researchers and clinicians that could be hindering the discovery of treatments. In the current Ebola epidemic in West Africa, for instance, much attention has been focused on the ill and the dead, even though crucial clues to curbing the outbreak may be found in those who remain healthy despite being exposed to the virus.
>
> Instead of focusing on what microbes do or do not do, researchers should ask whether an interaction between a host and a microbe damages the host, and if so, how.
> . . .
>
> Despite decades of searching, no classical virulence factor suitable for vaccine development has been identified for the tuberculosis bacillus or malaria parasite. Pulmonary tuberculosis occurs in less than 10% of the people infected with *Mycobacterium tuberculosis*. In these people, an over-exuberant inflammatory response destroys lung tissue. [In our post-Ferguson era, we might call this "over-policing."]

I am reminded of a conversation I have been having with my teenage son, about how truth in science keeps changing. We are so often so sure that we have, thanks to hard work and genius, finally discovered "the truth" and relegated to the dark past our ancestors' ignorance. And then, a few generations later, a new theory—e.g. germ theory—comes along and seems to deliver the truth once and for all, until it, in turn, is supplanted.

May I be allowed a brief detour into Nietzsche's *Jenseits von Gut und Böse* (Beyond Good and Evil), Section 31 (in Walter Kaufmann's translation):

> When the young soul, tortured by all kinds of disappointments, finally turns suspiciously against itself . . . how it tears itself to pieces, impatiently! how it takes revenge for its long self-delusion, just as if it had been a deliberate blindness! In this transition . . . above all one

takes sides, takes sides on principle, against "youth."
— Then years later one comprehends that all this, too, was still youth.

We come back again to medicine, as to our touchstone, and noting that Plato's Socrates invariably used medicine as his starting point for explorations of justice and "the good." Germ theory has given us the idea that, to keep from getting infected and sick, we should often wash our hands or use anti-microbial products. And certainly there is evidence that hand-washing can help prevent disease. But there is also a theory that children these days are more prone to allergies and other maladies because of their lack of exposure to external agents, because they don't play in the dirt anymore. And medicine has been exploring treatments that involve putting alien fecal matter into sick people in order to give them the microbes they need to be healthy. Casadevall and Pirofski speak of the "host-microbe" interaction, which can lead to flourishing or disease. What is important, we might say, is not opposed things—us and them, microbes and hosts—but relationships, systems. (A leitmotif of the present essay: our science is ever in dialogue with our times, our social and economic lives. In the industrial age, the nineteenth century, there were inputs and outputs; now we have service-based economies and the Web; we see the importance of relationships, computer systems, social networks.)

From a political perspective we may be led, by analogy, to conclude that it matters less who they are and who we are, and more what kinds of relationships we are able to enter into. (Though this, of course, is a function of who we both are.) And we may see here, too, the walls between them and us breaking down. Instead of attacking and defending, we may see how we are, inevitably, intermingling. We might think about successful and unsuccessful interminglings.

Almost finally, and with George W. Bush again in mind, I would note that, although this is not a focus of Casadevall and Pirofski's

"Ditch the term pathogen," that piece does touch on the matter of identity. Or what I am headed toward saying is that the whole host-microbe paradigm may be outmoded if not wrong. It has been said, for example, that in a human body—or in this labelled-human host for a whole variety of organisms—the thousands of different kinds of bacteria, fungi, and archaea outnumber the "human" cells 10 to 1. Apparently the majority of these organisms have been too poorly researched for us to understand the roles they play. However, communities of microflora have been shown to change their behavior in diseased individuals. The once "normal flora" begin causing problems.

This, we might say, is the greater fear of states or of their governments. Not that some fringe group will become enraged and violently act out; such behavior only strengthens the power of the state and of its police. (And Hoover is hardly the only law-enforcement official—in the United States, Russia, and elsewhere—who has sought to promote violence in order to increase his own power and capacities for repression.) But things fall apart when the normal flora—the Third Estate in revolutionary France; US college students during the 1960s—are at war with the organism of which they are an integral part. (In a documentary about the Free Speech Movement at my alma mater, the University of California, Berkeley, one of the students remarks that he and his fellow protesters—students at an elite university—had been supposed to become the managers of the system, of its major corporations and government agencies. But now they were its most outspoken opponents.)

A state cannot survive without soldiers and police willing to shoot, teachers eager to indoctrinate, and food deliverers, healthcare providers, and religious leaders willing to nurture, comfort, and restore. So, too, a body cannot survive without, among other things, its bacteria, fungi, and archaea. And thus it seems wrong to imagine, as we do, that some microorganism-less, exclusively human-celled "I" exists, has meaning. A hotel without guests is not a hotel. And perhaps a state in which too many of the members work for the police or in national defense, or whose borders are too strong—too impervious to alien ideas—perhaps such a state cannot long survive. And similarly for hegemonic economic systems (capitalism now) or religious institutions (the Roman Catholic Church of the Middle Ages). Survival depends on diversity.

I would also briefly suggest, or recall, that an "us" cannot exist without a "them." Our ideas of health depend on our ideas of disease; our ideas of what is external depend on our ideas of what is internal, integral. Freud notes in *Das Unbehagen in der Kultur* (*Civilization and its Discontents*) that the apostle Paul's idea of universal love as the foundation of a Christian community necessitated the extreme intolerance of this community—its savage attacks on outsiders. But we are back to something like germ theory here; Freud's perspective was a product of the nineteenth century. Now we can well imagine that wars within Paul's own psyche—as within J. Edgar Hoover's and many, many another's psyches—are what led to the hatefulness, and to a reduction of the world into a war between good and evil, and to the positing of the possibility of a good within threatened by the evil without.

IN MEDICINE, POLITICS, AND PSYCHOLOGY, we have had this idea that there is some "I," the host, who has an integrity and purity, and who is threatened and perhaps invaded and occupied by alien bacteria or bacteria-like agents, which may be helpful (undocumented alien cleaning ladies, nannies, and nurses) or noxious (ISIS, Al-Qaeda). In some religions there is the idea that the "I" may be born corrupt, and so one of its fundamental struggles is to achieve purity, by driving out the bad parts of itself. Such thinking helped "inform" and make effective the propaganda that led to the Holocaust. Jews, Leftists, trade-unionists, homosexuals, gypsies were labelled as evils within, and it was proposed that goodness and purity could be achieved by extirpating them: killing them.

This was of course worse than vicious propaganda, but my point here is that it was also bad "science," in the sense that current circumstances (our technology and economic systems included) are calling our attention to the extent to which there is no purity within; there is no "I" and them, no "us" and them. There is a collection of different entities that can and do relate in a range of ways, some of which are considered beneficial to the collection as a whole, and some of which are considered noxious.

Casadevall and Pirofski write that *Escherichia coli* (*E. coli*) is "one of the many species in the human gut," and that as a rule these bacteria cause no harm. Indeed, the traditional view is that these bacteria prevent the colonization of the intestine with pathogenic bacteria. But E. coli can also cause diarrhea and vomiting.

Again: we might do well to ditch the term pathogen, along with our fixation on evils beyond our borders or crossing them. We might focus more attention on our interminglings—when do they seem to work, and when not?

[16]
NRALGBTQ

ONE, BALMY SPRING WEEKEND, the National Rifle Association (NRA) held in Nashville a convention to which (television told me) 70,000 people came. My son and I were visiting our nation's capital and went to get a gelato at a capital gelato place. The person who served us was a tall, slender, quite-good-looking young man. He had long, blond hair neatly parted in the middle and with some strands held in a ponytail. Where his shirt opened there shone a hand-crafted medallion, held by a black cord around his neck. His fingernails were polished black.

The conjunction of these two scenes helped crystallize in my mind not only the connection between the NRA and the LGBTQ movements, but also a key aspect of American politics, and economics, of the past half century if not longer. Although this weekend saw the crystallization, parts of the idea had found places in my consciousness previously. In particular there had been another moment, a year or two earlier, when New York State Governor Andrew Cuomo approved gay marriage in the state and, at least temporarily, became a hero to millions of gays and lesbians, to their friends and family, and to liberals in general. I do not know remember which particular concomitant event led me to this understanding, but it was clear to me, as I watched the celebratory parade down Fifth Avenue, that there was a trade-off. We New Yorkers were not getting gay marriage for free. Specifically, I had the sense that the goodwill Cuomo was earning for supporting gay rights was going to be used to allow him to do favors for the real-estate industry. (E.g. Cuomo proposed that nothing be done that year to strengthen rent-protection laws. His public justification for this: turmoil in the state legislature as a result of federal probes into its corruption. It is worth noting that, of the New York state legislature, typically the corrupters are developers, landlords, and their agents.)

Schematically, the trade-off might be viewed as follows.

(And, I repeat, this is a schematic presentation, not an attempt to report specific facts.) In return for gay marriage, New York State's rent-stabilization laws could be a little weaker than they otherwise would be. Suppose this cost New York City renters an average of $100/month extra in rent, and suppose there are 2 million rental apartments in the city. The cost of gay marriage would then be $200 million per month, month after month, till death do us part.

Similarly, I assume that the gelato-server was enjoying a right that previous generations of ice-cream parlor workers did not enjoy: the right to dress for work in a non-heteronormative way. But he was, and likely without realizing it, paying a price for this privilege.

Let's suppose the difference was that the minimum wage was $1/hour lower than it otherwise would be and that this fact depressed wages for unskilled service-workers by an average of $1/hour across the board. That is, I am proposing, some number of politicians were able to get a certain number of votes thanks to their support for equal rights for people of all genders and sexual orientations and thanks to their opposition to discrimination based on gender or sexual-orientation. These votes—or, rather, the willingness of a certain bloc of voting-age citizens to go to the polls and vote consistently—allowed the politicians to make compromises with the business interests who were funding their campaigns, besieging them with public-policy papers and media noise, doggedly lobbying them, and ensuring them of wondrous lecture fees and high-paying private-industry jobs. Vastly simplifying, we are supposing that the compromise that was made was a $1/hour wage difference. And thus, if the cross-dressing gelato server was working twenty hours a week, his right to cross dress could be said to be costing him $20 a week, or about $1,000/year. And supposing the shop as a whole used 100 hours/day of unskilled service work, the acceptance of cross-dressing saved the employer $100/day, or more than $35,000/year.

In fact, the savings—or costs to renters, workers, et al.—are much larger than this. I remember, for example, when George W. Bush's Supreme Court nominees were being approved by the US Senate. Hillary Clinton and other Democrats focused the debate on where these people stood on the issue of abortion. Of course this is a major issue; many people value extremely highly the right of women to get an abortion. But it was clear to me that this focus on abortion was coming at the cost of a focus on where these nominees stood on business issues: occupational safety and labor-organizing laws, campaign finance, etc. It would take a sophisticated economist to come up with an estimate of how much money changed hands—moved from the working class to the business class—as a result of these Supreme Court appointments. And it may have been politically impossible for Democratic Senators to reject these nominees on the grounds that they were too pro-business. But what is certain is that the public was led, to include by Democratic Senators, to focus on the issue of abortion, and to not see clearly how much money—how much of their money—was at stake. And, I would propose, it has yet to be calculated how much the right to abortion has cost the working people of this country in lost wages, benefits, and legal protections. Again, this is not to argue against abortion, and particularly not in 2017 when, in the rightwing attacks on abortion rights, one can feel a desire to cripple women and to do this by taking advantage of the fact that women happen to have the vaginas and the wombs—for all of us!

NONETHELESS, THE POINT OF THE PRESENT PIECE is to urge knowing the prices of the social policies and rights that we buy or are sold. The fact that the NRA is befriended, and egged on, by rightwing rather than leftwing politicians makes less difference than people realize. Many NRA members work in low-paid jobs, too, and the fact that they are willing to go to the polls and vote consistently for politicians who support their right to bear arms—this allows a certain group of politicians to make compromises with the business interests who are funding their campaigns (and perhaps their life styles), besieging them with public-policy papers and media noise, doggedly lobbying them, and ensuring them plush lecture fees and private-industry jobs.

Underlying these dynamics are the dynamics of a modern,

mass "democracy." (That is, we are assuming "democracy" is still an appropriate term for such a political system.) Most people are disinclined to vote because they do not see much of a connection between the votes they cast and the nature of their lives. "I" do not feel I can go to the polls and make my life more as I wish it were. (And thus the act of voting is, in part, a humiliation.) The exception is or may be if I am part of a large bloc of voters that can be counted on to cast its votes for candidates who support some simple position: the right to bear arms, gay marriage, increasing or preserving social-security benefits. Such voting blocs have disproportionate influence because they stand in contrast to people who do not or may not go to the polls at all or whose voting choices are more diffuse. (There are, for example, those of us—worthless to the political process—who might, say, oppose a pro-gay-marriage politician because she has also been a real-estate-industry supporter.)

Complicating the matter are the business interests that fund the campaigns and the candidates. This fact—the power of money—means that the single issues that might give rise to a voting bloc cannot be working-class economic issues. The United States economy as a whole was at least as healthy fifty years ago when income disparities were much less than they are now. But we cannot successfully form a voting bloc whose single issue is, say, more progressive taxation politics—to share the wealth. We cannot form such a bloc because it will not have nearly as much money to pay candidates as the business interests have. The way current income inequality is likely to be readjusted is via another Great Depression, in the midst of which business interests will see that their customers need to have more money to buy their products and services.

THE GOAL OF THIS PIECE has been to call people's attention to two basic points. One is the hidden costs of social issues. We all are paying daily, and in ways we do not see, for the right to bear arms, to marry whomever we want, to get abortions, and many other things. Retirees can be counted on to go to the polls and vote for candidates who promise to preserve or extend benefits for retirees.

This does not simply cost non-retirees money because they end up paying for these benefits; they also end up paying for the hidden compromise, for how their candidates, once having preserved or increased benefits for retirees, are now also able to advance the quite different interests of the people and businesses who are giving them the most money.

Secondly, this piece has sought to call attention to how this dynamic is the same for putatively rightwing and leftwing causes. Our "democracy" provides ways for a well-organized, cohesive group to get what it wants on a social issue, but this getting comes with hidden economic costs. Of course this fact is hardly lost on the business interests who find ways to encourage the organization of social-issue-focused groups and who encourage candidates to cater to these interests.

[17]

In Kant's Wood

On freedom, competition, and the flowering of our species

> Among the early spring-flowering trees the dogwood, *Cornus florida*, is unrivaled in beauty. It usually grows 15 to 25 feet in height and is generally wider than tall. With fall comes a brilliant show of scarlet to reddish purple foliage and bright red fruit (drupes) borne in small clusters. The fruit often lasts into December or until it is devoured by birds. The flowering dogwood's natural habitat is under tall pine trees or on the edge of a deciduous forest. In this microclimate, dogwoods receive filtered sunlight, high humidity, and protection from drying winds. The leaf litter that falls each year benefits the dogwood's shallow root system.
>
> Adapted from an article on flowering dogwood posted on line by the North Carolina State University College of Agriculture and Life Sciences

THE MOST FAMOUS LINE of Immanuel Kant's essay *Idee zu einer allgemeinen Geschichte in weltbürgerlicher Absicht* (Idea for a Universal History from a Cosmopolitan Point of View) has been translated as follows: "From such crooked wood as man is made, nothing perfectly straight can be built." It may be noted that Kant's line echoes a wonderful line from Ecclesiastes, or from Ecclesiastes in English: "That which is crooked cannot be made straight: and that which is wanting cannot be numbered."

Ecclesiastes was more pessimistic than Kant, seeing little hope of progress or significant action. "All is vanity." "What profit do we have from all our labor under the sun?" Kant proposes, rather, that competition, by driving us trees and humans to labor as hard as we can, brings to us both a wonderful profit.

> Each needs the others, since each in seeking to take the air and sunlight from others must strive upward, and thereby each realizes a beautiful, straight stature, while those that live in isolated freedom put out branches at random and grow stunted, crooked, and twisted.

That is, we need others because they force us to work harder to compete with them, so that "I" survive rather than or better than "you." Even as you may be losing out, perishing for lack of light or water, you may also be helping me grow straight and tall. Were you not around I would feel more relaxed and dissipate my force in horizontal explorations and grow my flowers in unproductively whimsical manners. And were I not around, you would not, even in death, look so stiff (if not quite tall enough to have survived).

I trust that the information on *Cornus florida* suggests that the matter may be more complicated than Kant has proposed. "The flowering dogwood's natural habitat is *under tall pine trees* . . . The leaf litter that falls each year benefits the dogwood's shallow root system." "The fruit . . . is devoured by birds."

The present text will endeavor to imitate not Kant's conifers, but the flowering dogwood. That is, the piece will grow more wide than tall and benefit from the shade and litter of various philosophers and writers, while not ignoring the virtues of filtered sunlight, i.e. of the wisdom of some of Kant's observations and such other things as may be learned through an examination of Kant's wood analogy, or woods analogies, their contradictions included. For example, in Kant's sentence first quoted above we are forever crooked, while in the second sentence, thanks to the competition that a well-ordered society both encourages and regulates, we can help one another grow straight—i.e. realize our potential as human beings. Also enlightening in this regard is the dialogue between Kant's wood and Rousseau's state of nature in which we begin straight, and then, thanks to competition and other aspects of human society, we become bent and rotten. Kant, it needs to be noted here, was a great admirer of Rousseau; once, for example, praising him as the Newton of ethics.

I have worked on this piece over several months and on two continents, and to include within *le Palais-Royal* in Paris, at a restaurant table from which I could see through the straight, evenly spaced trunks of the trees to a gushing fountain, spreading its water like a *fleur-de-lis*. All of this is art, or music, but one of the points of this essay is that philosophy is not like that. Philosophers may imagine that they are seated at tables in a well-ordered park, but in fact they are walking through forests of light and shadow, of the crooked and straight clashing and climbing, flowering and rotting (and being devoured by birds). Each time one engages in the practice of philosophy one chooses a path, or, like the present piece, several paths, and while the paths, scenes, and trees can never be the same from one time to the next, the forest remains.

I WOULD TAKE A FEW PARAGRAPHS to note that the wood analogy is not all that is of interest in Kant's *Idea for a Universal History*. First and foremost, the essay paved the way for later explorations in the philosophy of history, and particularly for Hegel's and Marx's explorations which portrayed human history as having a goal: the full realization of the potential (real or imagined) of human nature. It is hard not to think, also, of the Nazi *Die Endlösung* (the final solution) in this context. And, with this and the two world wars in mind, it has been hard for me not to be put off by a few passages in Kant's essay, such as the one, not necessarily false, about how wars have the transcendent purpose of establishing new relations among states or such as the passage about how—

> Der Mensch will Eintracht; aber die Natur weiß besser, . . . was für seine Gattung gut ist: . . . Arbeit und Mühseligkeiten . . .

> Man wishes concord; but Nature knows better what is good for the race; she wills discord. He wishes to live comfortably and pleasantly; Nature wills that he should be plunged from relaxed, passive contentment into labor and hardship . . .

Some years of my money-earning life were spent working under a man who seemed to feel that it was his lonely but exalted mission to convert whatever remained of his multinational staff's relaxed contentment into *Arbeit und Mühseligkeiten* (labor and hardship). It always seemed to me that this man's effort had less to do with effective management, or with any deep understanding of the human predicament, than with an attempt to live up to, and a kind of dry thrill in living up to, the demands of a strict and unforgiving God. And I could not see that this God had anything universal or natural about Him; He seemed rather the product of the pinched vision of the boss's particular and not very happy subculture. We are not far here from Kant's vaunting of duty, his idea that human actions are good only insofar as they are motivated by a desire to act dutifully (obeying not the state or a denominated church, but a rational idea of the good).

WE HAVE ALSO TRAVELED A BIT FAR AFIELD and left the "Universal History" essay for *The Groundwork of the Metaphysics of Morals*. Returning to the essay under consideration, I note that near its conclusion, in its suggestion of a way for us to realize our potential, Kant's essay may be said to have—in 1784 and while leaving behind the putative advantages of war and discord—laid out the case for the United Nations. From the eighth of the essay's nine theses:

> In the end, war itself will be seen as not only so artificial, in outcome so uncertain for both sides, in after-effects so painful . . . that it will be regarded as a most dubious undertaking. The impact of any revolution on all states on our continent, so closely knit together through commerce, will be so obvious that the other states . . . will prepare the way for a distant international government for which there is no precedent in world history.

Kant's promoting of such an institution, backed by an ideal constitution, connects to two ideas of freedom. One of these ideas Kant, inspired in part by Rousseau, developed in his great *Critiques* (of Pure and Practical Reason). As the Kant scholar Robert Johnson has succinctly summarized the matter, for Kant, *Freiheit* (freedom) "does not consist in being bound by no law, but by laws that are in some sense of one's own making." The other idea is that the "free" behaviors of an individual can be noxious to his community and thus ultimately to the individual himself (or herself). "Free" here does not correspond to the Kantian sense of freedom just discussed, but to behaving in headstrong, self-centered ways, unconstrained by *Ordnung und Regeln, Regeln und Bestimmungen* (order and rules, rules and regulations). Because we human beings are more than willing to pursue our own interests and pleasures at the expense of other humans, Kant writes in his essay, we need "a master, who will . . . force us to obey a will that is universally valid, under which each of us can be free." Thus the central proposal of the *Idea for a Universal History*: in an ideal, universal government of our own devising we could find our greatest freedom, with "greatest" here in the sense of giving us the greatest opportunity to realize *alle ursprünglichen Anlagen der Menschengattung*: all the natural capacities of our species.

Kant further argues that the task of coming up with such a master of our own devising is not only essential for our species, but also next to impossible, since the master must be a human being or a group of humans equipped and controlled, by means of a constitution, so that he or the group acts not in a self-interested fashion, but to promote justice and the "freedom" of all. Socrates and his colleagues went down a similar path in *The Republic*, and so, too, James Madison and the framers of the United States Constitution. See Madison's writing in the fifty-first of the *Federalist Papers*, e.g.:

> If men were angels, no government would be necessary. . . . In framing a government which is to be administered by men over men, the great difficulty lies in this: you must first enable the government to control the governed; and in the next place oblige it to control itself.

In his speech at the Virginia convention to ratify the Constitution, Madison said: "I believe there are more instances of the abridgment of the freedom of the people by gradual and silent encroachments of those in power, than by violent and sudden usurpations." And the present state of US society offers sad support for Madison's arguments, as we see a wealthy, aggressive, anti-social few profiting overwhelmingly from the rest of the people's labor and loyalty, and justice is now an expensive commodity, available to those who can afford the requisite legal teams and the costs of buying an unimpeachable social status and a wall of social connections.

As regards universal government, the United Nations provides a concrete example of the problem Kant was wrestling with. The Charter of the organization features exalted goals, but these serve, inter alia, to disguise the extent to which the organization preserves and promotes the "self-interests" of established government, and, more particularly, of certain governments and their major stakeholders. Thus, for example, the Security Council's capacity to promote world peace is limited in part because its structure and rules seek to preserve and promote a particular set of international power relations: those leftover at the end of the Second World War. And "non-state actor" is, understandably, a term of opprobrium at such an organization of governments; yet realizing *alle ursprünglichen Anlagen der Menschengattung* depends in large part on such actors, be they popular uprisings against the encroachments of those in power, or labor unions or individual artists, or the environmental forces that keep crying out, but in an earthly language that state actors and their major stakeholders have difficulty understanding.

EXPLORING ANOTHER PATH, heading closer to Kant's forest analogy, it may also be well asked what laws of their own devising are tall-and-straight-growing trees obeying? Before arriving, finally, in this thicket, however, let us put two more possibilities in our rucksack. The first will emerge from a modern example of Kant's vision in somewhat successful action and the second from the most famous concept of Kant's *Universal History* essay.

The example is how in our present automotive times governments have been able to organize and regulate the private, public, and commercial use of motor vehicles so that qualified drivers over a certain age are able to enjoy the freedom of driving on roads provided by the state (i.e. by the tax dollars of the drivers or of the citizenry as a whole). Of course the system is far from perfect; here in the United States, tens of thousands of people are killed yearly by motor vehicles. The global figure is 1.2 million—yes, 1.2 million—deaths per year. Nonetheless, it is clear that the widespread use of motor vehicles would not be possible absent such a system, which includes infrastructure, regulations, driver's education, and social mores. In being incorporated into this system as we come of age we lose some of our freedom (in a non-Kantian sense; our freedom from constraint). We cannot drive at any speed in any direction, and in this regard it could be said that we (or the wealthier) were better off in the age of horses, except that while the overall freedom of movement may then have been greater, the speed and thus the geographical range of our movements was more limited. It is also the case that we can drive much faster than the speed limit, but only with the danger (and with the pleasure of the danger) of being fined or arrested and losing our driving privileges (to say nothing of the possibility of killing ourselves or others).

Extrapolating, we can say that Kant's approach champions a wonderful ideal: how a type of good government can increase the capacities enjoyed by all or many people. And, although our example has not focused on this point, such a government can also minimize the differences in the amounts of freedom or capacity-development-potential enjoyed by some individuals as compared to others. It could, for example, use tax policy or pro-labor legislation to ensure that no citizen's income was more than ten times that of any other adult citizen or that all schools, public and private, had the same amount of funds per pupil. Would such policies change the feeling in the United States from dog eat dog, every person for herself of himself, to something of less heat but greater warmth—a feeling of solidarity, of shared struggle?

Such policies would also, however, serve as yet another reminder that freedom from constraint is reduced in a system in which the "freedom" to develop one's capacities depends on rules, regulations, and socialization processes, however "good" (egalitarian or effective at capacity development) they may be. The mythical cowboy on his horse, more or less alone on a Great Plains, could wander wherever he wished (or wherever there was sufficient food and water), and at a gallop or a saunter. The suburban commuter may daily travel hundreds of miles—a daily distance that could put the cowboy to shame—but the commuter must travel on a prescribed set of roads, at a prescribed set of speeds, and in a complex harmony with other drivers, police, insurance companies, et al. (And in spending an hour or two on urban "expressways"—trying, for example, to get to New York's JFK airport from the center of the city, but 15 miles away—one may be led to reflect on how much more quickly some distances could be covered in the days before highways and the automobile.)

Kant's "famous concept" is human *Ungeselligkeit* (unsociability), or—better—the "*ungesellige Geselligkeit des Menschen*" (the unsocial sociability of human beings). With this phrase Kant is referring to our propensity, or indeed need, to enter into society, bound together with our wishes for autonomy and for freedom from constraint, which wishes constantly threaten to break up our societies. In 1927 the psychotherapist Alfred Adler noted that we human beings are forced to compensate for our weakness by forming alliances and cooperating, and this activity, far from relieving us of our feelings of deprivation and insecurity, embodies them. From Kant's more optimistic, late eighteenth-century perspective:

> Man has an inclination to associate with others, because in society he feels himself to be yet more human; that is, more in a position to develop his natural capacities. But he also has a strong propensity to isolate himself from others, because he finds in himself at the same time the unsocial characteristic of wishing to have everything go his way. Meanwhile he expects opposition on all sides because, in knowing himself, he knows that he, for his own part, is inclined to oppose others. This opposition awakens all his powers, brings him to conquer his inclination to laziness, and, propelled by vainglory, lust for power, and avarice, to achieve a rank among his fellows, whom he can neither endure nor do without. Thus are taken the first

> true steps from barbarism to culture, which contains all that is of value in human society. Here all man's talents are gradually developed and his tastes refined; through continual enlightenment the beginning of a foundation is laid for a way of thought which can in time convert man's coarse, natural disposition for moral discrimination into definite practical principles, and thereby change a society of men driven together by their base instincts into a moral whole. These characteristics of unsociability, which each man can find in his own selfish pretensions, are in themselves quite unattractive and give rise to conflict. But without them all human talents would remain hidden, unborn in an Arcadian shepherd's life, with all its concord, contentment, and mutual affection.

"[H]is fellows, whom he can neither endure nor do without"—I have much appreciated the sophistication of such observations of Kant's. In speaking to a psychotherapy patient, Adam Phillips once noted a similar oddity—this "sense we can have that other people are the ones who spoil the things we can't actually do without them."

At the time I began work on this essay I was also reading *Le Mariage de Loti*, Pierre Loti's Romantic view (first published in 1880) of life in nineteenth-century Tahiti.

> In Oceania, work is something unknown. The forests by themselves produce all that is needed to feed the carefree people. Breadfruit and wild bananas grow for everyone and leave no one unsatisfied. For the Tahitians year follows year in the midst of a perfect idleness, a never-ending dream, and these great children have not the least idea that in our beautiful Europe so many poor people exhaust themselves, striving to earn their daily bread.

Loti himself sets these idyllic moments off against reports of sadness and melancholy, in the quiet and isolation of these far-off islands and with the population slowly succumbing to European diseases and domination, the beautiful girls naïvely embracing a life of prostitution. And thus we could return to Kant's observations with yet greater assurance that in the long run the potential of our species will not be realized by those of us who (like Loti's Tahitians) give up fishing because the climate is not conducive to working and because they can live on fruit and thereby have more time for napping, bathing, and making love. Or, say, we could take a twenty-first-century Pascalian view, from which Loti's novel would help us yet better understand the noise and commerce of Western life, its *Arbeit und Mühseligkeiten* and its United Nations included. All this, a Pascalian can observe, may have less to do with our realizing our potential, than with finding ways of diverting ourselves, of blocking out the sadness, of avoiding having to appreciate and accept the human predicament.

WE ARE NOW MORE THAN READY to return to the wood and the trees. Let me quote again, and at greater length, from Kant's forest analogy:

> It is just the same [for we humans as it is] with trees in a forest: each needs the others, since each in seeking to take the air and sunlight from others must strive upward, and thereby each realizes a beautiful, straight stature, while those that live in isolated freedom put out branches at random and grow stunted, crooked, and twisted. All culture, art which adorns mankind, and the finest social order are fruits of unsociableness, which forces itself to discipline itself and so, by a contrived art, to develop the natural seeds to perfection.

With help from all the spade work we have done heretofore, let us explicate or extricate this. Were each of us to develop on our own, we would indeed end up with crooked branches (like an apple tree?), and this because we would enjoy some kind of—unimaginable for those living in complex societies?—constraint-less freedom. Interestingly, one way of looking at the resulting problem is that such freedom would leave us goal-less. On any given day we might grow in any direction or several or not grow at all, and without there being any notable consequences beyond our twistedness. We might find the results agreeable or not as we wished. Imagine the proverbial ten chimpanzees being set to the task, not of reproducing Shakespeare, but of playing roulette, and with this one qualification: no matter what number they placed their chips on, that number won. A bit like Loti's Tahitians, the chimps would be offered low-hanging fruits or expectationless caresses. Some of the chimps might end up demoralized, with nothing demanded of them and it making no difference how they played the game. Some might additionally, passively, reason that since the 17, say, always won, they should keep playing that number. Others might follow a more "twisted" path, reasoning that since all numbers appeared to be winners, why take the trouble of being consistent, or why not enjoy the pleasures of throwing one's chips on the board helter-skelter? (*Cf.* Montaigne's description of himself as *un "ennemi juré d'obligation, d'assiduité, de constance"*: a sworn enemy of obligation, constancy, and perseverance. A fitting position for someone who had seen the ball land squarely on his number—for an heir to rich and productive estates which he was able to leave to the management of his wife and other capable people.)

Kant's idea of how we humans grow straight and tall, however, has little to do with my chimpanzee analogy, nor with Montaigne. For Kant (a short man, by the way), straightness and tallness are most certainly the goal, and they are hardly easy to achieve, and any success will owe nothing to chance. Straightness and tallness are forced on us or on the trees by competition (e.g. for sunlight). Being naturally vainglorious, avaricious, and power-hungry—*ungesellig* (unsociable)—our fellow humans or trees would take all the sunlight they could command for themselves, elbowing the rest of us aside, stunting our growth or leaving us to starve to death (or reducing us to begging or prostitution—the role of the dogwood?). These are not uncommon outcomes in human societies, and we could say that for human beings they can be horrible, but Kant's proposition is that there is also something invaluable, even wonderful, here. None of us would grow straight, nor would we be able to enjoy our wonderful artistic and intellectual productions, were we, our artists and philosophers included, not subject to this competition—were we not forced, in order to survive, to grow as straight and tall as possible.

In the United States of recent times this would be called a neo-conservative position, and it may lead some to recall Social Darwinism as well. The survival or flourishing of the fittest is not only a good deal for those who may happen to find themselves most fit for surviving or flourishing in the circumstances in which they find themselves; the system works for most everyone. The exception is those disabled, challenged, defective, victimized many or few who lack the genes, motivation, or faith in straight-growing that are essential for success. Of course they are not going to find it easy to survive, but the remaining many or few, by being forced to be as fit as they can possibly be, may indeed end up being as fit as they could possibly be.

That's the theory in any case. And Kant's forest analogy may help us begin to perceive its weaknesses. Different species and genetic make-ups of trees grow straighter and taller (and in different soils, different climates, and lights), but are the straightest and tallest in any given forest the best? Not say, if one likes or depends upon edible fruit. And would you prefer a forest of firs straight and tall which you could fell in order to build homes and railroad ties, or a deciduous, "old growth" forest featuring many different kinds of trees, oaks for building, apples for apples and dogwoods for their early spring blossoms, their drupes, etc.? And by applying mulch around all or some of the trees (or by judicious pruning?) could we promote an increase in the sizes of a wide range of trees and increase, too, the fruitfulness and beauty of the whole forest—and this much more impressively than if we simply left the trees (or humans) alone to elbow aside others or to themselves be elbowed aside? (And where is The Lorax, who speaks for the trees?)

This is also the place for asking if my idea of a complex environment, different types of trees growing in harmony, is in fact the fantasy of someone who has spent vastly more time in New York's carefully tended Central Park than he has in any forest? And we can also ask if we—or some of us, yet not others—prefer our gardens carefully designed and tended in the French classical manner, the manner of *le Palais-Royal*—offering different flowers in different seasons, and many signs of constraint but none of dying or decay? Or do we prefer the wilder English gardens, or simulations of luxuriant wildness such as in the landscaping of Manhattan's High Line "aerial greenway"? Or—best of all?—a walk in autumn woods, climbing over fallen logs and circumventing patches of mud and stagnant pools? Or do we like (and dislike?) all of these things and at different times, depending upon our mood and circumstances (the state of the economy included?)?

Any answers notwithstanding, I will now turn to another aspect of Kant's analogy. As I worked on this essay, I recalled reading that Kant had but one picture on the walls of his home: a portrait of Rousseau which was hung over his writing desk. This memory was connected to a sense that a Rousseauian version of the forest analogy would be quite different. For Rousseau the "natural seeds" (e.g. of human beings) do not need to develop to perfection; they are perfection. The conditions under which these seeds are forced to grow—human society with all its unsociableness certainly included—corrupt the innocent young saplings. Kant proposed that from such crooked wood as man is made, assuming that he is not helped to grow straight either by a just master or by competition, nothing perfectly straight can be built. A Rousseauian version would be: The straight wood that humans might be we will never be because, being social animals, we are forced to live in society, and society is inevitably corrupting.

And now we (with Rousseau's help) are far from any neo-conservative or laissez-faire approach to government. A young child in some ideal, never-existing state of nature (or in a state free from regulations, taxes, subsidies, public education) may be perfect and pure, if also quickly eaten by wolves. She has in any case no choice but to be raised in society—so as not to be eaten and because she is a member of a species that learned, eons previously, to stick more or less together, and this at least in part in order to survive. And so, while surviving, a young child is also quickly corrupted by social customs and ways, forms of government included, and to such an extent that she soon becomes herself part of the corrupting force. (And all this while little aware of how her habits, thoughts, and feelings continue to be shaped by social forces.)

Let us pause here to note that the semi-Rousseauian vision of the Tahitis and Tahitians of the world is that they existed for millennia in an ideal, childlike state, free from predators, to include from the temptation to prey on one another, until The Fall: the arrival of Europeans. In this vein, Loti remarks on more than one occasion that Tahiti is one of the rare countries in which one can sleep outdoors, exposed to the elements, without fear of predators (or, say, without getting too cold). From one perspective, the fact that one cannot do this in Europe is what has made us "Westerners" taller and stronger (in limited senses of those two words) than the Tahitians and others, and thus has led to our global hegemony. From another perspective, Loti's peaceful Tahiti is itself a European fantasy. As a powerful man may dream of powerlessness or wish to act this out (for example, in sex play), so Loti and many another Westerner, arriving on their invading ships, wished to find peacefulness and to play at it, to include during sensual interludes with the locals.

I have also read, in *Nature*, that our species' survival may have less to do with our competitiveness or, say, the size of our brains or our ability to band together, than simply on the high rotational velocity our shoulder muscles are able to achieve.

> Some primates, including chimpanzees, throw objects occasionally, but only humans regularly throw projectiles with high speed and accuracy. Darwin noted that the unique throwing abilities of humans, which were made possible when bipedalism emancipated the arms, . . . [O]ur throwing capabilities largely result from several derived anatomical features that enable elastic energy storage and release at the shoulder. ("Elastic energy storage in the shoulder and the evolution of high-speed throwing in *Homo*," 27 June 2013)

This might lead to a further conclusion: a few (species or individuals within species) succeed not because circumstances force them to, but because, from birth, they enjoy advantages over others.

In harmony with the contradictions of Kant's essay, the present text continues to present opposed possibilities. Thus, on the one hand, let us observe how parents, teachers, and other adults are wont to say that education, socialization included, is for children's "own good." And in so saying they (or we) skip over what may be most essential in all the teaching: gaining protection (e.g. in the form of professional degrees) from wolves, human and otherwise, and being trained in how to make successful use of one's own aggressive instincts. Our children are at some pains to learn how to find the rotational velocities and the projectiles—be these marketing strategies, computer algorithms, land ownership, laws, capital, particular symbols of social status—appropriate to our moment in history. As modern parents we do not spend much time teaching our children to throw and dodge literally speaking, but, nonetheless, more of their education than we may wish to admit may come to this: throwing and dodging. And insofar as our hypothetical young child is able to absorb and make use of this education, she may become more striker than struck, more consumer than consumed.

Alternatively, Rousseau and Kant hold out hope for the possibility of a society that—*grâce à* some kind of *contrat social*, in the Rousseauian view, or some kind of *Verfassung* (constitution) in the Kantian view—could regulate the freedom, security, and indeed innocence of each and every child and adult so as to promote the maximum freedom, security, and innocence for all. So that, notwithstanding our self-interests and aggressiveness—or, better, by harnessing such things—each of us can be as free, secure, and uncorrupted as possible, and notwithstanding our aggressiveness, mutual dependence, and frustration (and rage) at our clawless (and often clueless) vulnerability, at our having to depend on and even help others, and at all this coming in the end to naught but death for each and every one of us.

Le pauvre en sa cabane où le chaume le couvre

>   Est sujet à ses lois,
>
> Et la garde qui veille aux barrières du Louvre,
>
>   N'en défend pas nos Rois.

(François de Malherbe, "Consolation": The poor man in his hut, with thatch for cover, is subject to death's laws; nor can the guards at the gates of the Louvre protect our kings from them.)

Arrived, finally, in the thicket of Kant's woods analogies, let us focus on the tension or contradictions. Is Kant's view ultimately Rousseauian: natural forces would not only let us but indeed force us to grow straight, were it not for the confusion (the darkness?) of the forest in which we, as social animals, live and grow? Or was Kant in his *Idea for a Universal History* rejecting Rousseau for some variation on the doctrine of original sin and the slim or slimmer hopes thus offered? It is not possible for trees to work together to redesign the forest in which they grow—to prune themselves, as it were—and it would seem almost as difficult for the fundamentally crooked to conspire to bring straightness to their own lives; but we might still hope that, were such wonders possible, were our prayers answered, we and our offspring might grow straight and tall, enjoying a no longer corrupted will thanks to the perfecting forces of a now ideal society?

The wood and forest passages appear in the middle of Kant's text (a German fairy tale of dark woods and with the happy end always beyond reach?). Further along a reader may discover that the whole text is not meant to be an analysis, prediction, or proposal so much as a kind of fantasy or "mere idea," a *focus imaginarius*. This Latin term and the notion that philosophical examinations may involve such mere ideas appear in the *Critique of Pure Reason* and not or not quite in the "Universal History." In the latter work Kant presents his exploration of the possibility of a perfect constitution, of human beings learning to master themselves and their instincts, as a way above all of resisting pessimism, of clinging to hope—of clinging to the hope that Nature or God has a plan, a good plan, for our species. In the ninth, concluding thesis he writes:

> If, further, one concentrates on the civic constitutions and their laws . . . a guiding thread will be revealed. It can serve not only for clarifying the confused play of things human, and not only for the art of prophesying later political changes . . . , but for giving a consoling view of the future (*which could not be reasonably hoped for without the presupposition of a natural plan*) . . . . [The italics are mine.]
>
> Such a justification of Nature—or, better, of Providence—is no unimportant reason for choosing a standpoint toward world history. For what is the good of esteeming the majesty and wisdom of Creation in the realm of brute nature and of recommending that we contemplate it, if . . . we are forced to turn our eyes from it in disgust, doubting that we can ever find a perfectly rational purpose in it and hoping for that only in another world?

This is an interesting and not uncommon approach to philosophy, in which the psychology of the philosopher, his or her faith included, becomes the basis for an analysis or argument which is couched in the rhetoric of rationality and which by and large avoids making reference to the matters of faith or to the author's psychology, and for all these latter may be said to provide the real justification for what are otherwise hollow claims. Wishing cannot make it so, one would like to reply.

THIS PIECE IS TITLED "IN KANT'S WOOD," and I would like to leave us there, or here, in this forest of his and ours. I believe that I have shown that it is a tangled and dark or dappled place. And thus tempting and satisfying and frightening to explore.

Afterword — Of making much of trees there is no end

A colleague, having read a draft of the above essay, recollected weeks spent on an estate in Kent, England, an estate situated in the midst of apple orchards. The grounds

> had expanses of lawn, ponds, and topiary hedges. The orchards occupied much land beyond the estate. In the evening we would wander among the trees, picking fruit as we wished. But I noted that few of the old free-growing apple trees remained. Most were cultivated to a shorter, wider sameness that facilitated picking.

This is to say, among other things, that the exploration of the present essay is but a beginning. The farther we go, the farther we can see and the more we realize that the view is inexhaustible. As Bakhtin (or his translators) put it: "The world of culture and literature is essentially as boundless as the universe. We are speaking not about its geographical breadth (this is limited), but about its semantic depths, which are as bottomless as the depths of matter."

[18]
The Beauty of the System

A good deal has been written about tobacco, drug, oil, and other companies—companies that have worked to deny or raise doubts about scientific information suggesting that their products were lethal or had profound environmental consequences. What I am waiting to see is writing about (and by) the people who work in these companies or for the companies contracted to provide advertising and public relations, or expert analysis. I would like to see an article by one of the historians at Yale, Oxford, and Ohio State who apparently took hundreds of thousands of dollars from the tobacco industry to promote "moderate view[s] of substance use," as one phrase has it.

How does it feel to do this work? that is my question. How does it feel in the first phase when you have seen data suggesting that the product you are putting on the market—Vioxx, for example—increases the risk of heart attack by 400 percent as compared to a competing pain reliever? And how does it feel in a second phase when it becomes publicly known that your company hid or ignored such evidence? (In Vioxx's case, it is estimated that in five years the product caused 100,000 heart attacks, of which 30 to 40 percent were fatal.) We are talking here about thousands, likely hundreds of thousands, of workers, not only in the tobacco, drug, and oil industries, but lots of others of us. (There are those, for example, who in providing one or another form of technical support to one or another neo-colonial international organization, play their miniscule role in driving subsistence farmers off their land and onto the fringes of megalopolises where there may be only garbage to eat and polluted water to drink.)

In an article on "Manifested Uncertainty: Contested Science and the Protection of the Public's Health and Environment," David Michaels, a former US Assistant Secretary for Environment, Safety and Health, in addition to providing the statistics on Vioxx given above, quotes from the website of a public relations company—a sentence in which the company boasts about how it was able to undermine and counteract the scientific evidence indicating that phenylpropanolamine (PPA), once widely used as a decongestant and appetite suppressant, caused strokes. But again, Michaels is writing about deceptive research and public relations, and about deaths, but not about this matter of feelings—the feelings of the people involved in turning other people into victims. That one was, that we are, paid to do such work may be the best excuse. We did it for money, more than one bank robber has proposed. Harder to excuse is the consequence, the 100,000 heart attacks, or the 200 to 500 strokes a year (among 18 to 49 year olds) that were caused by PPA.

The text that follows does not take on the subject as it is described above, but a yet larger one.

WORRIED THAT YOU MIGHT HAVE CANCER, twins, a herniated disk, you go for a high-tech medical test and afterward ask the technician what the test has revealed. The technician says she cannot say; the testing facility's doctor will need to look at the results. In a few days this doctor will send your doctor a report.

Annoyed, if not enraged, you curse the American medical system. Just so doctors can get rich and enjoy a feeling of superiority they don't deserve, or just because there's a whole 'nother batch of cannibals getting rich off malpractice lawsuits, you—the one who is paying and worrying—have to wait. And, from what you've seen of the images and numerical printouts, the test doesn't seem all that difficult to interpret, and this technician has a great deal of experience. You can see in her face that she already knows—you do have cancer, or twins.

In your anger and anxiety you are ignoring the beauty of the system. This technician—for all she can indeed see exactly what you have and don't have—does not trust her judgment. She could misinterpret the test, she thinks—not that she can recall ever having done so. She could be missing something. She is certain the doctor knows more and is smarter than she is. She had not needed her teachers to remind her; she had learned this lesson before starting school.

Two neighboring countries have been fighting for years over an infertile spit of land that lies along their border. Resources desperately needed for teachers, schools, vaccines, antibiotics, food, and water are being spent on fighter jets and anti-aircraft missiles. Hundreds of soldiers and civilians are being killed every year or maimed by landmines; crops are being destroyed; women and children are being raped and enslaved by marauding troops—with no end in sight.

Frustrated, if not enraged, you denounce the cynicism and heartlessness of politics. The leaders of the two countries are perpetuating this war, and fanning the flames of chauvinism, demonizing the enemy, imprisoning critics as traitors—and they are doing this to keep their long-suffering people from turning against them, to divert attention from how they and their friends are looting and mismanaging the country's resources. And meanwhile the leaders and diplomats of major world powers continue to publicly condemn the senselessness and brutality of the war, and also continue to do whatever they can to help businesses in their countries make money manufacturing and selling jets, missiles, and landmines to both sides.

In your anger and idealism you are ignoring the beauty of the system. Among the many soldiers who are dying in this gruesome charade of a war, there are those—perhaps even the majority—who believe that they are dying for a great cause. Grieving mothers, while wishing that somehow the bullets might have found them instead, find comfort in the thought that their sons did not die in vain.

What with all the media tells us about concentration camps, sweatshops, and migrant workers, corporations knowingly exposing their employees to toxic products or fouling rivers and communities with them, it is easy enough to wonder: What sort of human beings could choose, or even accept, to make a living abusing and killing other people in such a way? How can people be so cruel? How can such people live with themselves?

And we hardly need the news and history books to set us to wondering. The other day I met a real-estate agent who had talked an old, single woman into selling her desirable house and property and buying a smaller place in a barren part of the county where no one was eager to live. His reward: commissions on both the sale and purchase. One of the most pernicious pollutants is the used motor oil that millions of ordinary individuals pour or allow to leach into the ground. I remember a colleague who, jealous of a writer working in our office, began telling the boss that in between tasks this writer was sneaking off to work on his essays. How many big and little stories we all could tell. And in moments of honesty each of us can certainly also recall when we have been the exploiting, polluting, or backstabbing one.

But in the midst of such thoughts let us not forget the beauty of the system, which is that the office rat does not think she is a good person, she knows she is one, and she would be glad to tell us why. She is not depriving a writer of a means of earning a living, but helping an important organization, helping a good boss, helping her other colleagues who, unlike the writer, are fully committed to their jobs.

The slum landlord is proud that he is one of the few people willing to provide housing to the poor. Many who kill animals for sport and sport alone believe they are providing a valuable service, thinning animal populations, protecting farms, gardens, and drivers on the highways, saving later animals from starvation. And like most people—like cigarette-company executives who support the arts, or the artist whose art work offends the residents of the city where it is displayed—the hunter doesn't simply think he is providing a service, he wants to be thanked.

An entrepreneur goes into the hills of some poor country and gives peasant families cash in exchange for their teenage daughters and sons. A monster, you might call him, ignoring how he is providing peasants the cash they need to get out of poverty, ignoring how he is providing thousands of European and American sex tourists a few hours of much-needed fun, ignoring how he is providing the children a chance to come to the big city and try to build a better life. He may adjust the children's schedules and loan them some money so they can go to school in their spare time. The beauty of the system is how it works for everyone.

[V]
Closing Words

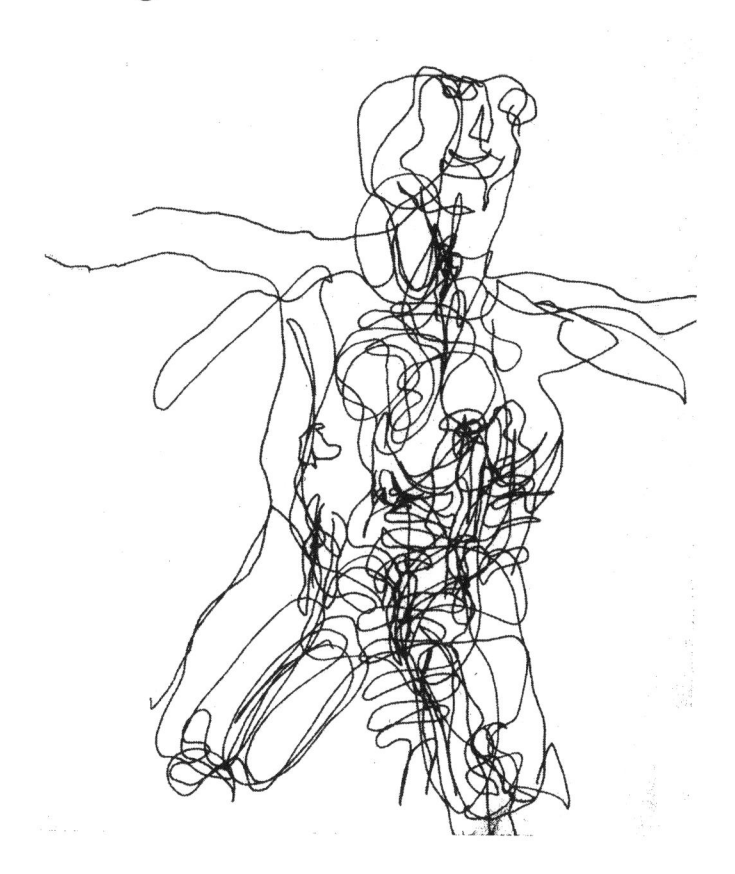

MAYNOTTHETRUTHBERATHERTHAT
DESIREISTHECAUSEOFFRIENDSHIP
— from Plato, *The Lysis*, here in a pseudo-original form

[19]
Sonnet for 9/27

On cherche un partenaire, mais seul l'amour peut nous trouver.

> *One looks for a partner but can only be found by love.*

Puisque la recherche empirique emploie plus de gens que les activités plus intellectuelles, peut-elle avoir tort ?

> *Since empirical research employs many more people than more intellectual pursuits, can it be wrong?*

Nous sommes sur la bonne voie pour mourir de rires préenregistrés.

> *We are on pace to die of canned laughter.*

Le chien comme qui je travaillais.

> *The dog that I worked like.*

Ce qui n'est pas vraiment souhaité est très difficile à trouver.

> *What is not really wanted is really hard to find.*

Grâce au langage, le rapport mots-caresses est devenu défavorable aux caresses.

> *Thanks to language, the ratio of words to caresses has gotten out of balance.*

Une chaîne est une chaîne est une chaîne.

> *A chain is a chain is a chain.*

Le dernier versant non développé est couvert de poésie.

> *The last undeveloped slope is covered with poetry.*

Notre rage n'est plus acceptable, même à nos propres yeux.

Our rage is no longer acceptable, even to ourselves.

La lame de son décolleté

The blade of her cleavage.

Pour nous il n'avait plus d'intérêt parce qu'il était donneur plutôt que preneur, et les donneurs se retrouvent assez vite sans plus grand chose à donner.

We lost interest in him because he was a giver not a taker, and givers quickly end up with nothing left to give.

Il est plus facile d'être tué sur l'autoroute que par un terroriste.

It's easier to get killed on the highway than by a terrorist.

« Taisez-vous ! » lança-t-il à l'instructeur qui lançait aux enfants de se taire.

"Be quiet!" he yelled at the instructor who was yelling at the kids to be quiet.

L'allaitement pourrait bientôt être tout ce qu'il nous reste.

Breastfeeding may soon be all that is left.

[20]
Bologna Postmodernism Bob Perelman Amis

> If it tastes good we eat it.
>
> A sister who points to the sky at least once a decade is a good sister.

ONE OF THE LAST ROOMS of the Museo della Storia di Bologna takes up the subject of language. I do not know why this subject occupies one of the last rooms, beyond Bologna's hidden canals and Marconi. The exhibit has included a video of two men drinking wine and speaking two dialects of the region, choosing phrases that emphasize the differences between these two dialects.

I can develop a theory as to why I spent more time watching this video than I did with the mortadella machine (broken the day I visited) or in the rooms devoted to the Catholic Church, Napoleon, or the founding, in 1088, of the first university in the history of the world. My theorizing would begin with my interest in languages and with the importance of the physical act of conversation to Italians, the pleasure of speaking. Equally important was my guilt—at having passed through this museum at a rapid pace without engaging or being engaged. Before reaching the end, I felt obligated to stop at something.

Readers may also wish to know at some point that - 30 - has been traditionally used by journalists to indicate the end of a story. There are many theories about how the usage came into being—e.g. in the mid-nineteenth century, the number 30 was telegraphic shorthand to signify the end of a transmission. Also significant—not that such a word, nor "importance," fit comfortably in a text such as this one; yet here they are, and I am calling it significant that I had come to the museum of the history of Bologna more or less direct from New York, having slept an hour or two on the plane, half an hour on the express train from Milan. I had not travelled from New York to see this museum. Eager for a break from my New York routine, I had more or less put a finger on a map. And then, after arriving at my hotel near the Bologna train station, I had read in a guidebook an enthusiastic recommendation of the museum. And each room of the museum included one-page sheets describing the exhibits. The pages in English were usually missing from the racks; more often I found Italian, French, German or Spanish. And I read many of these pages—on the diagonal, as the French say (skimming).

That afternoon in the Museo della Storia di Bologna, I was happiest in the café, with a friendly waitress and one of Kingsley Amis's comic novels: *Girl, 20*. Amis's alter-ego was making his first visit to a Sixties discothèque in London:

> A girl clad in a piece of silk measuring at least eighteen inches from top to bottom appeared through the gloaming and gave out sheets of vellum which I took to be menus. I peered hard at mine, polished my glasses on the paper napkin provided, peered again and made out phrases . . .
>
> Half a minute later we were on a small dance floor. . . . The majority of couples were performing at rather than with each other, making rope-climbing or gun-shot-dodging motions with an air of dedication, as if all this were only by way of prelude to some vaster ordeal they must ultimately share.
>
>> You look great in shorts. And the flag looks great too.
>>
>> Even the words floating in air make blue shadows.

I WISH TO TELL OF MY TRAVELS less in Bologna than in our postmodern world. How do we go through lives in the absence of a central narrative or objective; perhaps creating meanings and values by our actions, our juxtapositions; perhaps not?

Before boarding Delta 418, I had been reading Frederic Jameson's much-travelled essay, "Postmodernism, or, The Cultural Logic of Late Capitalism." Depth, he was telling me, was being "replaced by surface, or by multiple surfaces". And all modern culture is now characterized by "autoreferentiality . . . which tends to turn upon itself and designate its own cultural production as its content."

When I got to Il Museo della Storia di Bologna, a receptionist offered me an audio guide, free, in English. After standing several minutes in the initial space holding this thing to an ear, I gave it back. Too slow.

The woman in the gift shop got angry with me for my putting the machine back in its place in the box of audio guide machines and for trying to repossess my ID card myself. This was against the rules.

And of course the museum offered no central narrative. I have wondered, subsequently, if this is not, among other things, a way of avoiding the problem of political incorrectness—or the problems that may result from taking any position at all. If no connections or causes are asserted, or if any such are left for each viewer to assemble on his or her own, who (but perhaps me, thinking the rules, too, irrelevant) can be accused of anything? In "Within the Context of No Context" (1980), George W.S. Trow writes: "In the New History, nothing was judged—only counted. The power of judging was then subtracted from what it was necessary for a man to learn to do."

I often have the sense, too, that we have now arrived in the Dark Ages of capitalism. The institutions and dogma of our times so enclose us that we are not only losing a capacity to judge, but also to imagine alternatives. (In Jamesonese this becomes: " . . . a certain minimal aesthetic distance . . . the possibility of the positioning of the cultural act outside the massive Being of capital . . . distance in general (including 'critical distance' in particular) has very precisely been abolished in the new space of postmodernism.")

> We live on the third world from the sun. Number
> three. Nobody tells us what to do.
> But better get used to dreams.

MEANWHILE, I NEVER FOUND OUT why Bologna? Why a city here? And why, from a relatively long view, has this particular city been so extraordinarily successful? I am prepared to say—and not only on account of the delicious *seppia* (cuttlefish) and Veneto wine that I enjoyed on the Via Broccaindosso—that Bologna is one of the most successful cities in the history of the world. Though the recent economic downturn has weighed on it, Bologna has long been very wealthy. In 1256 the commune of Bologna became perhaps the first governmental body to abolish slavery and release the serfs. The text of the law (known as *Liber Paradisus* [Heaven Book]) famously states: « Paradisum voluptatis plantavit dominus Deus omnipotens a principio, in quo posuit hominem, quem formaverat, et ipsius corpus ornavit veste candenti, sibi donans perfectissimam et perpetuam libertatem ». (In the beginning God planted a paradise of delights, where he put the man whom he had formed, and adorned his body with a bright dress, giving him the most perfect and perpetual freedom.) Wikipedia also tells me that during the Renaissance Bologna was the only Italian city that allowed women to excel in any profession they wished to take up. "Women had much more freedom than in other Italian cities; some even had the opportunity to earn a degree at the university."

Location, location, location—that's my hypothesis. Geography is destiny.

In the Amis novel, *Girl, 20*, a famous conductor and violinist is leaving his second wife for a girl not yet 20, and yet younger than his second wife had been when they first met and the composer had become enthralled by her youth and had left his first wife. There's a central narrative, or old story, and traditional values here—fear of mortality, the eternal attractiveness of youth; the youth of others, and even of young products (smartphones, etc.) helping one deny or ignore one's mortality. The second wife goes over to the new girlfriend's apartment in order to confront her. One of the girlfriend's responses is to strip off all her clothes, to show that she has a more attractive, more youthful body than the become-middle-aged second wife. "You're not . . . capable of loving!" the wife yells.

"Maybe I'm not," the girlfriend says. "You could have a point there. . . . But anyway, it doesn't matter, that side of it, does it? Whatever I'm like he prefers me to you and that's why he's leaving you and going off with me, and that's all there is to it. He wants to and I want to, so that's what we'll do."

Values do not shape our actions, our actions create values, the opportunism of which may make them seem valueless.

> The sun rises also. I'd rather the stars didn't describe
> us to each other; I'd rather we do it for ourselves.
> Pick up the right things.

IN AN EARLIER DRAFT of this piece I made much of how the exhibits at Il Museo could be compared to phosphorescent plankton. My sense of such beings is that they only give off light when they happen to collide with something, or when something, such as a human limb, happens to collide with them. Either the force or the friction leads to light. I could be wrong. I am not a marine biologist, and I am not going to Google. I do not mind being wrong. And my point remains: our haphazard collisions can create a kind of light that rarely lasts long. (And I remember, hardly for the first time, long hours spent in Quaker meeting, alone at the far end of a bench—my chosen spot—waiting for The Light to reach me, as it were through the long, white mullioned windows, but without the least collision, force, or friction.)

Http://www.genusbononiae.it/index.php?pag=25(accessed on Veterans Day, 2015): Il "Museo della Storia di Bologna rappresenta un percorso museale dedicato alla storia, alla cultura e alle trasformazioni di Bologna, dalla Felsina etrusca fino ai nostri giorni. . . ." A journey dedicated to history and culture of Bologna from Etruscan times to our own . . . recounted in an innovative way using interactive, etc., technology . . . The splendid cornice of the medieval palace reinvented . . . and the layout . . . make a visit to the museum a unique experience.

> Hey guess what? What? I've learned how to talk.

Great.

It's always time to leave.

Closing note: The lines between each section have been chosen, not quite at random, from "China" by Bob Perelman, a poem first published in *Soup #2* (1981). Like other readers, I first encountered this great work in Jameson's "Postmodernism" essay, in which "China" plays a central illustrative role. According to Jameson, Perelman, strolling through a Chinatown, "came across a book of photographs whose idiogrammatic captions remained a dead letter to him . . . . The sentences of the poem in question are then Perelman's own captions to those pictures, their referents another image, another absent text; and the unity of the poem is no longer to be found within its language but outside itself, in the bound unity of another, absent book."

[21]
Friendship, Deception, Writing
Within and beyond Plato's Lysis

1

Plato's dialogue the *Lysis* concerns friendship, and it is possible that it is this—friendship—that has, above all, eluded and frustrated scholars and led to the low regard in which the dialogue has been held. Of course, this is not how the scholars themselves would tell the tale. "[N]ot positively instructive or helpful," one has written. Another: "without positive result . . . speakers and hearers more puzzled than they were at the beginning." Prominent nineteenth-century classicists proposed that Plato had not in fact written the *Lysis*, because it was full of sophistry and eristic (arguing for the sake of scoring points, winning an argument). Others proposed that the dialogue was made up of *adolescentiae vestigia*—stuff written when Plato was quite young. A leading twentieth-century scholar's verdict: The text "is not a success. Even Plato can nod."

The *Lysis* is a story, told by Plato's Socrates, of a conversation he had with two naked boys while a third, slightly older boy, half hidden, watched and listened. The ostensible *philosophical* objective of this conversation was to come up with a definition of friendship, and this objective does not *seem* to be achieved. That is, instead of an answer to the question "what is a friend," most of the *Lysis* wrestles inconclusively with various received ideas of who is a friend to whom, how, and why. This wrestling is tiresome because, as in arid academic discussions, Socrates, at least as he tells the story, seems to have lost touch with his feelings and desires—for friendship, for connection. It might be said that these desires underlie all of the conversations of Plato's Socratic dialogues, and it may be for this reason, yet more than because of the intellectual challenges the Socrates character and his interlocutors navigate, that so many of the dialogues seem to come up short, or fail to arrive at the truth they were seeking. Intellectual dialogue can be a poor substitute for something warmer, which we would like to call friendship.

At the end of the *Lysis*, Socrates, with seeming or feigned cheer and self-mockery, recounts how he told his young interlocutors, as their chaperones led them away from him:

> If neither the beloved, nor the lover, nor the like, nor the unlike, nor the good, nor the congenial, nor all the other cases we went through—I can't remember them all now, there were so many—If none of these are friends, I don't know what more to say. . . . O Menexenus and Lysis, how ridiculous that you two boys, and I, an old boy, who would like to be one of you, should imagine ourselves to be friends . . . and yet we have not been able to discover what a friend is.

2

I would not have wrestled long and hard with the present set of notes if I shared the traditional view of the *Lysis*. Indeed one of the objectives of these notes is to encourage fresh readings of the dialogue. And more: I would like to encourage fresh thinking about friendship and about writers' intersections with it and with their craft more generally. As either Plato or I am the principal writer concerned here, we—along with the dialogue's characters: Socrates, Lysis, Menexenus, and Hippothales—will provide the examples of friendship, and its absences and discontents.

In the end friendship is our great topic—and a great topic it is. Our experiences with friendship and our yet greater longing for friendship play large roles in our lives. As regards Plato's work, these notes will propose that in the *Lysis* Plato, for various possible reasons, has intentionally hidden beneath the surface much of what he has to say about friendship, as well as many of his feelings about and experiences with friendship. And yet, I am proposing, at least in this case, Plato's greatest insights may be uncovered by readers less concerned with logic than life.

3

I could be the first reader of the *Lysis* to imagine that it could be speaking, in part, about the isolation, however delicious or productive, of a writer's life. I am not the first to have noted the leitmotif of deception that runs through the text. For example, Christopher Planeaux, a Plato scholar, has called attention to Socrates's statement in the very first line: "I was on my way from the Academy, making straight for the Lyceum" (i.e. from one leading gymnasium to the other). Planeaux has proposed that this statement is immediately contradicted by Socrates's own description of his route, which, as Athenians of Plato's time would have recognized, was not direct. (A caveat: at that time, few of the approximately 250,000 Athenians could read or were interested in the written word. Plato may be thought of as writing works for the amusement-stimulation-education of members of his club and a few affiliated "clubs" in other parts of the Mediterranean.)

It is possible that the keyword here should not be "deception" but "indirection." Socrates is after something, but he cannot pursue it directly. And, as regards writing yet more than friendship, note that if Plato had more interest in "direction," he would not have written dialogues and stories about dialogues that may or may not have taken place.

Let us stick for the moment, however, with the idea of deception, which is also of friendship as deception. It quickly raises the question of who the Socrates of the *Lysis*, the principal friend/deceiver (misdirecter), is or is supposed to be. Here, too, we may find ourselves deceived. In Plato's time, "Socrates" became the name of a stock character, written about by many writers. They used, played with, and extended the traits with which this character became associated. A similar thing occurred in Spain with Goya, who, after his death, was turned into the embodiment of an ever-evolving collection of Spanish values.

Given the current solemn approach to Plato's dialogues and his homely-looking Socrates, the readiest comparison may be to what "Honest Abe" has become in American culture. But, as the classicist Kenneth Dover has noted, "[T]he Greeks were often arbitrary, impulsive, frivolous, cynical, witty or jocular, and they are not always well served by too earnest or solemn a temperament in a modern interpreter." We may do better to compare the Socrates character to Paul Bunyan or to the Native Americans' Trickster, who, for example, once extended his penis from one side of a lake to the other in an attempt (failed, I believe) to have sex with maidens bathing on the other side.

In the *Phaedo*, Socrates is described as sitting chatting on his deathbed with two visitors from out of town (think of the Three Stooges or of Groucho, Harpo, and Chico). No sooner has one of the visitors recalled Socrates's idea that learning is recollection than the other interrupts: "But how is that proved? Please remind me, as I can't quite remember at the moment."

When Plato's Socrates starts the *Lysis* by claiming to have taken a direct route, and when it is clear that, in fact, he is once again heading to a gymnasium—where good-looking boys are naked—and when he then begins worming his way into their company, we may imagine Plato's first readers nodding their heads and chuckling, "Typical Socrates." (A scholarly note: the Greek word "gymnasium" is formed from the Greek for nude: *gumnos*. Along with being social clubs, the Athenian gyms trained boys to wrestle.)

4

The Plato scholar Ann Michelini, discussing features of the stock Socrates character, notes in particular his *eirôneia*, his exaggerated claims of weakness or incompetence, made in order to deceive. At the gymnasium Socrates seeks out Lysis and his friend Menexenus—young aristocrats, best friends, about thirteen years old (to Socrates's fifty or so). Socrates tells the boys that his interest in friendship stems from the fact that he has never been very good at making friends. Plato's first readers may have laughed aloud, as this claim flies in the face of evidence from the Socratic literature and many of Plato's dialogues that one of Socrates's great talents was making friends (in some sense of this word). Indeed we might say that, like many another hanger-on, Socrates's greatest problem is his penchant for making friends even, or above all, with people who are more good-looking, well-born, and powerful than they are nice or well-intentioned. Socrates, the son of a midwife and a mason, has a grand time with his rich and powerful young friends, until the traitorous, disastrous actions of a few of them lead to his being sentenced to death (the charge: corrupting Athenian youth).

Even just reading the text of the *Lysis*, as if we had read no other dialogue, we are unsure what to make of Socrates's claim that he is not good at making friends. Does he imagine he is telling the truth? Or is he having some fun? Is this a tired line of an aging sexual predator? Like a spin serve in tennis or like some of the "spinning" in politics and public relations, Socrates's deception serves to move his pubescent interlocutors out of position, far from the truth and thus more vulnerable to future assertions.

5

"I was on my way from the Academy, making straight for the Lyceum," Socrates begins, falsely. Assuming that there are texts with relatively reliable narrators, we can wonder if the *Lysis* could be the first text in Western history to make use of an unreliable narrator, a narrator whose unreliability is revealed at the start of the narration and is a deliberate creation of the author. And if so, why did Plato decide to take, or explore, such an approach in this text? Was he wishing to call attention to how in friendship we are always dealing with people who misrepresent or misunderstand themselves? Was he wishing to question how we can indeed become friends with such people? With whom—with which of these mirages— would we become friends? (Aristotle argues that our best friend is, or should be, ourselves—another veteran deceiver.)

In the *Phaedrus*, Plato's Socrates says—disingenuously? or is Plato poking fun at himself when he has Socrates say—that, unlike dialectical conversation, writing cannot "teach the truth adequately." With this in mind we can also imagine that, with the *Lysis* and its unreliable and somewhat ridiculous narrator, Plato was not trying to teach, but, first and foremost, amusing himself.

Early in the *Lysis*, Socrates, speaking to Lysis alone, gives him a demonstration of *elenchus* (refutation via cross-examination), convincing Lysis that, until one has knowledge, one cannot do what one wants. (If you do not know what you are doing or should be doing, how can you ever do what you want?) More radically, Socrates also convinces the thirteen-year-old that if, as a result of our ignorance, we are useless, no one, not even our parents, will love us. Plato then has Socrates pause in his narration to remark on how impressed Lysis is by his (Socrates') arguments, and, when Menexenus rejoins the group, Lysis asks Socrates to "say what you've been saying to me to Menexenus too." He wants his best friend to have the same experiences as him or to be similarly put in his place, revealed through *elenchus* to be quite ignorant.

In the translation I own, Lysis's request comes at the bottom of a recto page. My first time through there was a delicious moment when, before turning the page, I entertained a hope that Socrates would in fact do, or report doing, as he had been asked—that he/Plato would give the same discussion all over again, offering the pleasures and insights of hearing the same story told twice. Next, upon turning the page, I wondered why Plato dangled before our eyes this possibility but let it go. It brings to mind Shakespeare in *A Midsummer Night's Dream* having "the mechanicals" rehearse one set of lines in one act and then, later on, perform a different set. The literary critic Harold Bloom has written of Shakespeare (in *Love's Labour's Lost*) seeming "to seek the limits of his verbal resources, and [discovering] that there are none." I had the sense, at this moment in the *Lysis*, of a gifted writer, near the beginning both of his own writing life and of the literary age, noting—for himself, above all, and in the midst of glimpsing how truly gifted he might in fact be—*What might I [Plato] not do were I to make use of all the bells and whistles of this writing thing?* (An answer: the *Symposium*, where so many of the bells are rung, so many of the whistles blown.)

6

In the *Lysis*, Plato contrasts the innocent, unknowing, pure friendship of Lysis and Menexenus with the world of conniving adults, a world in which even the ostensible pursuit of knowledge, or of love, can become a kind of stain, a means of getting the better of others, or of seducing or misleading them into meeting one's needs. Socrates ostensibly enters into conversation with Lysis so as to show another person, Hippothales, how to talk to his beloved in order to win his love, or his allegiance at least. (Hippothales is either in love with Lysis or is pretending, to himself first and foremost, to be in love with him.) In Socrates's story of his day at the gym, the result of Socrates's demonstration is that Lysis becomes enamored of Socrates, hanging on his every word and not even noticing Hippothales, sitting off to the side. (Deception, like dialogue and dialogue-writing, involves diversion in both senses of this word. Deception and dialogue—conversation—lead us along indirect routes and also entertain us, helping us turn our thoughts from the one end at which we must, sooner or later, arrive.)

Before Socrates—making straight for the Lyceum—runs into him, Hippothales has been writing speeches and poems and singing songs in praise of Lysis. Socrates brings to light the bad faith and self-serving aspect of such behavior. "I," in singing another's praises, am glorifying *my* love, an object that *I* am going to win or lose. And furthermore, Socrates points out, the behavior is not effective, as it makes the lover and his suit, however poetic they may be, yet weaker. "When a man praises or compliments handsome boys," Socrates observes, "they become filled with pride and conceit. . . . And the more conceited they are, the harder they become to catch." (Here again, Plato's Socrates knows well whereof he speaks. In the *Charmides*, speaking about his judgments of the looks of boys, he remarks: "I'm nothing to go by . . . because pretty well all pubescent boys seem beautiful to me.")

Socrates's critique of Hippothales's purported pursuit of Lysis is that, if you would win the love of another, and particularly the love of a younger person not himself invested in feeling superior or in caring for the weak, you need to show him (or her) that you are at least his equal—or, better, his superior. There are two ways to do this: one is by making a show of your own capacities (e.g. by winning a wrestling match); the other is by making your beloved feel inferior. If he or she is young, beautiful, and rich, and you are, like Socrates, none of these things, then you might, for example, lead your beloved to feel stupid, uneducated, or tongue-tied compared to you. And thus he may feel you are worthy of being loved and may be anxious to try to impress you and win your love, and he may also feel that it is worth spending time with you, in order to gain from you what he himself so clearly lacks.

In the *Charmides*, Socrates is confronted with another very good-looking, well-born, and wide-eyed young man. The conclusion of the *Charmides* is, like the conclusion of the *Lysis*, aporetic; the conversants are unable to come to an understanding of what they had, at least in theory, set out to understand. But, nonetheless, the handsome young man, Charmides, overwhelmed by a sense of his ignorance and dazzled by Socrates's wit and intellectual force, expresses a need for Socrates's further teaching and a willingness to submit to it daily, "until you [Socrates] say I have had enough."

7

Socrates deceives (or recounts how he deceived) Hippothales by using the opportunity to demonstrate how to talk to one's beloved as a means of trying to win for himself, rather than for Hippothales, Lysis's affection. We may compare Plato's dialogue with *Cyrano de Bergerac*, in which an aging, ugly, noble soldier gives all his poetry and all his love for Roxanne to a young, good-looking man, Christian, who, in theory at least, is going to use these gifts to win her love and lips. A writer may well cry along with Cyrano when he reveals himself to his beloved, to whom he is, as we say, "just a friend."

Oui, ma vie

Yes, my life,

Ce fut d'être celui qui souffle, – et qu'on oublie !

> The one who puffs and pants and is forgotten.
>
> *Vous souvient-il du soir où Christian vous parla*
>> Do you remember the evening when Christian spoke to you
>
> *Sous le balcon ? Eh bien ! toute ma vie est là :*
>> Under the balcony? All my life is there,
>
> *Pendant que je restais en bas, dans l'ombre noire,*
>> Remaining below in the dark shadows.
>
> *D'autres montaient cueillir le baiser de la gloire !*
>> For others the ascent, the glorious embrace!

Note further how in both works the aging lover's demonstration also involves deceiving his beloved. Cyrano leads Roxanne to think Christian capable of beautiful poetry and devotion. Socrates gives Lysis the impression that he is speaking with him in order to educate him; hidden is Socrates's superficial project, to educate Hippothales, and Socrates's desire to win Lysis's affection for himself.

Or are we all deceived? Socrates is not a sexoholic, but an eduholic: he cannot help trying to educate every attractive, well-born young man he runs into. And what is Socrates's goal in seducing/educating Lysis (and Menexenus)? Is he actually seeking to become *proton philon* (an object of their love) or is this, too, a deception?

Men and women of many an era have enjoyed seducing others either for the simple pleasure of the seduction or to feel or demonstrate their attractiveness and power. From Molière's *Dom Juan*:

> *On goûte une douceur extrême à réduire . . . le cœur d'une jeune beauté—*
>
> It is an exquisite pleasure to conquer . . . the heart of a young beauty . . . to combat . . . the innocent modesty of a heart loath to surrender; to overcome step by step all the little obstacles that she sets in our way; to overcome the scruples on which she prides herself; and to

lead her gently to the desired place. [It is worth noting the inversion; in "real life" it is the woman who has the "desired place," and she may or may not wish to lead the man to it.]

In French the word *déception* is the equivalent of the English "disappointment." This can remind us that, in many lands, people are seduced by others who are, as we say, just playing games, and how, as a result, sooner or later the seduced may be not only deceived but also disappointed, demoralized. They may well come to find, and likely not for the first time, that what was deficient above all was *philia* (attraction) itself. (Another scholarly note: In the context of the *Lysis*, φιλία [*philia*] has traditionally been translated as "friendship." It can also be translated as "attraction," "attachment," or "love"—e.g. *philosophia*, love of wisdom.)

The seduced may come to decide that the seducer was not really drawn to "me" or interested in any kind of ongoing, more open-ended relationship, in a real, flesh-and-blood exploration of friendship. (How many people are?) About Socrates we might imagine Lysis saying some days later, "I thought he wanted to be my friend, but it was just talk."

8

Socrates proposes to show Hippothales how to speak to Lysis in order to get what he (Hippothales) has been playing at wanting: love, attachment, sex. In setting out in this way, Socrates is not only taking an indirect route toward coming to understand friendship, he is plunging himself and Hippothales into what I will call lovelessness, into a cold world in which attachments are the products of manipulation or in which, for example, your parents love you if and only if you are useful to them, say, by being particularly accomplished, good-looking, or doting.

In the *Ethics*, Aristotle says that Plato used to often ask, "Are we on the way to or from first principles?" Are we now prepared to imagine Plato saying this with a smile, more amused than concerned? Or we might imagine that when Socrates first told Plato the story of his day at the gym, flirting with the beautiful, rich, naked boys by talking to them about friendship, at some moment Plato interrupted, "Are we on the way to or from first principles here, Socrates?" More earnestly, we can read Plato as asking us, his readers, if in our own pursuits of truth and friendship we are headed toward or away from these things—toward or away from truth and friendship?

Within the *Lysis*, Socrates appears to take another wrong turn when he engages Lysis and Menexenus in a seemingly frank conversation, and about friendship no less, without either discussing his interest in becoming intimate with them or revealing his ostensible ulterior motive: to demonstrate something to someone hiding in the wings. Plato is offering his readers a lesson in the *Realpolitik* of friendship: Socrates's befriending (helping) one person, Hippothales, involves the deceiving of others. To paraphrase Kant, from such crooked beginnings, nothing straight can be made.

9

We can hardly be surprised to find that, at the end of the *Lysis*, Socrates's behavior has left not only Hippothales in the lurch, but philosophy and Socrates himself as well. Socrates's professed desire is to leave the gymnasium with the two rich and attractive boys, but "suddenly," he recounts in the final paragraph, "we were interrupted by the chaperones of Lysis and Menexenus, who like evil spirits came upon us with the boys' brothers, and told the boys to come home, as it was getting late." (Wealthy Athenians tasked slaves with keeping their sons from being drawn by older men into conversation and from mixing with older teenagers at the gym. Socrates had wandered over to the Lyceum on this particular day because it was a holiday, a day on which older men were allowed into the clubs and got to see the boys.)

Getting to see naked boys—this, Socrates achieved. His winning of the argument and of Lysis and Menexenus' friendship, however, appears hollow, the friendship now seeming, like many a friendship, to be rooted in wishful thinking. At the end Socrates is left alone with what can be a feeling of uselessness—nothing but a story to tell. It is no accident that, unlike others of Plato's texts, the *Lysis* has no implied audience. It feels as if the narrator, Socrates, is telling his story to no one. And the melancholy is deepened by the fact that this telling is done in a jaunty tone.

10

Why does Plato's Socrates tell this story, which, though amusing, hardly puts him in a good light? And why did Plato go to the trouble of creating and setting down this story that does not put Socrates in a good light and that seems to end so inconclusively? Was it, as we have earlier imagined, simply a way of exploring "this writing thing"?

We might begin with the supposition that, in addition to the pleasures of exercising his writer's craft, Plato wanted to say—or get off his chest—some things about friendship. He certainly succeeds at showing us how in our friendships we may have various ostensible goals—seduction, sex, power, social climbing, seeing ourselves (however correctly or incorrectly) in a pleasant light—but it is while pursuing these goals that we get what we may most need and enjoy, even if we are not willing to fully admit this need and pleasure. I would define this *what*—this essence of friendship—as a kind of rubbing against other human beings, a rubbing and being rubbed by them. This analogy may seem more appropriate to sex or wrestling (and to the retirees who play paddleball every day at my YMCA), but certainly conversation, too, is a contact sport. And the warmth of its rubbing may be felt at most every intellectual and social level, and whether our conversations are deceptive, disappointing, and self-deceiving, or not.

It is not uncommon for a French person, over dinner, to try to provoke an argument with someone else, who will in turn take the bait so that soon these two, and perhaps the whole group, will be going at it, arguing with one another. To an American such conversations can seem disconcerting, even threatening. Until one recognizes the pleasure that lies underneath—the pleasure of this vigorous intellectual rubbing against other people.

11

If Socrates went to the gym to enter into conversation with naked boys . . . Well, for my part, as I was working on these notes in a New York City café, attractive young women were passing by on the street and coming in to get their mochaccinos, iced lattes . . . . It being a hot and humid summer, and fashions being what they are or were at that time, these women were, less or more, stripped down to their boxers, short shorts, and bras.

Socrates was not in fact interested in sex. He wanted the boys to be young and rich and beautiful and naked, but then he wanted to talk philosophy with them. In my case, I was *trying* to stay focused on my writing and rewriting. And among the distractions was an awareness that these women were prepared to take offense, if not go to the police, were I to propose that we might together and in a more private location explore either their wardrobes or what a word like "friendship" or "*philia*" could mean.

Which is all to say that these women were helping me appreciate how discussion and writing can be asked to satisfy deeper needs or desires—the need for rubbing, or friendship, perhaps first and foremost. And I can appreciate, too, how discussion and writing fail to do this, and how a talker's or writer's response to this failure is often to talk or write more. This is not the only alternative (there is alcohol, onanism, prostitution, figure-drawing, or tango classes), but words on top of words can seem the best one. If a life without erotic exploration with someone tantalizingly other (and tantalizingly similar too) at times feels not worth living, then a life well-examined can seem both a pale shadow and the next best thing. Third prize would be a life examined in yet greater depth, or over and over again.

12

The name Plato (roughly, "The Broad") sounds like a Robin-Hood-y nickname, and we have scant evidence of the life or character of the person so nicknamed. As one scholar, George Boas, has summarized what the data allows us to conclude:

> He [Plato] was highly praised by his successors in the Academy at the time of his death. He was probably born in 427 and died about 347 [BC]. (We know from the *Dialogues* the name of his father and of two of his brothers.) The rest is legend, no detail of which can be traced back to a date earlier than the second century A.D.

(And what does knowing "from the *Dialogues*" mean, insofar as they are inventions, works of fiction?)

This reality has not stopped scholars and popular writers from writing biography after biography of various Platos. And as Ulysses S. Grant remarked regarding fantasies about what actually transpired at Appomattox, some fictions "are told until they are believed to be true." In Plato's case, many of the biographies rely heavily on a letter that Plato probably did not write and on the confused collection of tidbits offered by Diogenes Laertes, who is often treated as if he knew people who knew Plato, whereas, in fact, one of the very few things we know about Diogenes Laertes is that he wrote more than half a millennium after Plato, *perhaps* in the first half of the third century AD.

As often in cases of *philia* (attachment) to another person, we are here entangled in and distracted and inspired by our projections. This "we" must include the author of this essay as much as anyone else, though I believe it is different when one knows one is projecting, when I accept that "my" Plato is some part of myself—either a part I do not wish to own up to or a part of me that I would like to imagine was also a feature of the life of a great philosopher.

That said, I will further propose, and now as pure speculation, that the portrait of friendship that lies half-hidden in the text of the *Lysis*—friendship as some mixture of disingenuousness, of deception, and of an ultimately sad playfulness, and of competition and erotic desire—all this *could* hold in greater darkness Plato's experiences with "friendship" or with other people more generally. And we might conclude that these experiences were not very pleasant or satisfying, but the kinds of experiences that could drive someone to write. Something, we can say, must have driven Plato to write with the necessary level of dedication, to give the number of solitary hours required, to produce a *Lysis* or, say, *The Republic*.

I have read that Plato has been thought to have been shy. I do not know in what century after Plato's death this idea was cooked up, but, *from the dialogues*, it *feels* right. In reading the opening of the *Symposium*—in which the writer ("Plato") intricately prepares one of his characters, who was *not* at a wonderful party years prior, to begin telling what he has heard about this party from someone who went uninvited—along with the word "playful," the phrase "painfully shy" comes to mind. In a rare autobiographical allusion, in the *Phaedo* Plato has a character remark that Plato did not join the others in attending on Socrates the day Socrates drank the hemlock, the last day of his life. This, we are told, is because "Plato was unwell." ("Social anxiety disorder" is a current phrase.)

A fair amount of recent scholarship argues that, the existence of written texts notwithstanding, Athens in Plato's time was not what we would consider a literate society. Legal practice, for example, was oral and independent of documents, and prose was written to be read aloud, be this in a relatively cozy space or in an amphitheater. If books were copied and sold, it was so they could be read aloud in other cities. Setting this down, I have intimations of violation (Plato's work being read aloud by strangers). A more recent technology, photography, has led some to think that when we take or show people's picture, we steal from their souls. But, of course, showing may have been Plato's goal. Perhaps the whole point of his isolation, like many another writer's, was so he could carefully imagine and craft something to show to others—to friends, fellow seekers of understanding (philosophers), or the public at large.

"You show me yours, I'll show you mine"—a saying associated with childhood attempts to learn about the opposite sex or about The Other more generally. One thing that makes writers and other artists seem different from other adults—and yet hardly unlike people who spend a great deal of time shopping for clothes and getting dressed and made up—is the lengths to which we go to develop some "I" or some artwork we are willing to show to others. (And instead of showing ourselves.) Some of us writers may end up *appearing* naked, but, in fact, we are always traveling under the cover of words, speaking through an authorial voice, not our own.

13

Freud proposed that the successful artist "is an incipient introvert who is not far from being a neurotic." Like so many others, an artist wants to achieve *Ehre, Macht, und Liebe der Frauen* (honor, power, and the love of women), but seems to lack a means of doing this. However,

> If he is able to make it possible for others . . . to obtain solace and consolation from their own unconscious sources of gratification . . . he wins gratitude and admiration for himself and so, by means of his imagination, achieves the very things which had at first only an imaginary existence for him: *Ehre, Macht, und Liebe der Frauen*.

Freud is focused on *being loved*: the successful artist is to be loved by others and such love is his goal. The *Lysis*, as I have suggested, spends a good deal of time on the question of who is attracted to or befriending whom, the lover or the beloved, the successful or aspiring, etc. Ideally, I would propose, friendship and love involve mutual attachments and pleasures, so that, for example, the truly successful artist would not only find lovers but would also find, in himself or herself, a capacity to love.

This puts in relief how solitary and self-contained Plato's project seems to have been. In a famous passage in the *Phaedrus*, he has Socrates, the great conversationalist, say that "in the garden of letters" a lover of wisdom

> will sow and plant, but only for the sake of recreation and amusement. He will write his thoughts down as memorials to be treasured against the forgetfulness of old age, by himself, or by any other old man who is treading the same path. He will rejoice in beholding their tender growth; and while others are refreshing their souls with banqueting and the like [while others are enjoying love and friendship, we might say], writing will be the pastime in which the writer's days are spent.

What Freud does not consider in the "incipient introvert" text quoted from above is the extent to which art-making can become an end in itself, one of *die Ersatzbefriedigungen* (compensatory satisfactions), as he elsewhere calls them. Given the deceptions and *déceptions* of human social life, rather than wishing to win honor, power, and love, a writer of dialogues, or essays, may find more than a little satisfaction in his imaginary friendships, in his rubbings on papyrus (or tapping on keys). As has been suggested regarding the great Portuguese writer Fernando Pessoa, one of whose aliases once referred to himself as God: if your imagination is so powerful it can people the world, there may be no need for actual people.

14

In Freudian psychotherapy and its offshoots, a session lasts a pre-established number of minutes. The time limit is thought to help us, as mortality sometimes does, to focus our thoughts and come to insights we would not otherwise come to. By contrast, in Lacanian therapy there is an idea that a patient comes to a session with one thing he or she wants to say, a statement she wishes to make to the world or the therapist, something she wants to hear herself say or get off her chest. In a pure form, a session of such therapy ends the moment the statement has been made (or when the therapist believes the statement has been made—or has to go to the bathroom? meet someone for lunch?).

We have just about come to such a Lacanian moment, for both me and Plato, and yet I would put it off with one last scholarly note. The earliest extant copies of Plato's dialogues come from the ninth century AD, more than 1,200 years after the original Plato (let's call him) died. We are reading, translating, analyzing, ruminating, and speculating about echoes—copies of copies of copies of . . . (Here's a loneliness.) As one of the experts, T. H. Irwin, has written, we cannot reasonably suppose that our versions of Plato's texts "contain all and only the very words that Plato wrote." This may be better appreciated if I add this detail from Irwin's history of the Platonic corpus:

> Copies of Plato were originally written in capital letters ("uncials"), without punctuation and without spaces between words. Small ("miniscule") letters were introduced, probably in the eighth century, and eventually punctuation was also introduced.

I mention this here because I will now, in closing, call readers' attention to one more deception—perhaps the greatest deception—in the *Lysis*. We, like many others, have noted that the dialogue ends inconclusively, with Socrates's quip about how he, Lysis, and Menexenus have not been able to figure out what friendship is. But it is possible that neither the fictional narrator Socrates nor the writer Plato really believed this. Once again they may have been only pretending, to auditors and readers and perhaps to themselves as well.

Just before the dismissive, self-mocking end, Socrates poses a series of questions that seem to sum up, and with not a little emotion, what has been learned, rightly or wrongly, as a result of his discussion with Lysis and Menexenus. I would have these questions stand also as the Lacanian statement of Socrates's story, of Plato's text, and of the present essay:

MAYNOTTHETRUTHBERATHERASWEWERESAYING

JUSTNOWTHATDESIREISTHECAUSEOFFRIENDSHIP

In other words, as I, on the heels of many another, have reconstructed it: May not the truth be rather, as we were saying just now, that desire is the cause of friendship? And that he who desires, desires that of which he is in want? And that of which he is in want is dear to him?

[22]
Sontag, Hell, Thinking, Politics

> To designate a hell is not, of course, to tell us anything about how to extract people from that hell, how to moderate hell's flames. Still, it seems good in itself to acknowledge, to have enlarged, one's sense of how much suffering caused by human wickedness there is in the world we share with others. Someone who is perennially surprised that depravity exists, who continues to feel disillusioned (even incredulous) when confronted with evidence of what humans are capable of inflicting in the way of gruesome, hands-on cruelties upon other humans, has not reached moral or psychological adulthood. — Susan Sontag, *Regarding the Pain of Others*

MANY EDITORS AND WRITERS have been thinking that—as the Chernobyl nuclear disaster may give rise to new forms of life?—the disaster of the 2016 United States presidential election will lead to new kinds of writing. The general ideal seems to be that *content* will be—should be—different. As if to say, No more fooling around. Or no more musing, sophistication, post-modern literary games—and no more celebrity profiles? Factored somewhere in here must also be a larger development: how electronics have changed people's reading habits, turning us into breathless skimmers, quickly plucking some possible gist before skipping, asap, to other posts. How—what?—does?—I write for such an audience (which includes me)?

Which is to say that the *style* of writing must change, too. At an extreme, during some post-election phase, this would be because fascist repression was so aggressive it was no longer possible to speak directly. Like La Fontaine at the court of Louis XIV, it would be necessary to resort to analogy.

Sire, dit le Renard, vous êtes trop bon Roi ;

Sire, the fox said [to the lion], you are too good a king;

Vos scrupules font voir trop de délicatesse ;

Your scruples reveal too great a delicacy.

Eh bien, manger moutons, canaille, sotte espèce,

You know, eating sheep, the riff-raff, fools—

Est-ce un péché ? Non, non. Vous leur fîtes Seigneur

Is this a sin? No, no. You do them, My Lord,

En les croquant beaucoup d'honneur

In munching on them, a great deal of honor.

Or, quite alternatively, there is the prose style that Donald Judd developed for talking about art in the early 1960s. "Most of the work in this show is different from [Claes] Oldenburg's other work and is even better. It is some of the best work being done. . . . I think Oldenburg's work is profound. I think it's very hard to explain how." And it is hard to see any current use for mannered approaches, but, on the other hand, keeping things simple and not quite getting straight to the point—why not?

In any case, changes in texts' content or style cannot be mandated, though they will be driven, half by the muses that guide and bewitch writers and half by writers' opportunistic responses to friends', editors', publishers', agents', and reviewers' evolving preferences. We may also feel confident that initial assessments of the "new writing" will give way to later, divergent ones. There was a time when Baby Boomers and Baby-Boom observers thought that the generation was being shaped by political protest, sexual liberation, and anti-conformism, and now we find that silicon chips and the increasing mobility of financial capital have played larger roles.

All this may come to seem an odd introduction to the paragraphs that follow since, in both content and style, these are much like the work I was producing before the election. And yet, as I believe readers may appreciate, the present text is indeed a post-election work. For this reason: it is a product of how the election results, and my and others' post-election mood, affected my *reading* of a pre-election text. Specifically, read in late November, early December 2016, *Regarding the Pain of Others*, Susan Sontag's second book on photography—published in 2003 as a kind of sequel to her highly successful 1977 *On Photography*—did not and could not seem to be about photography. This subject receded, while quite another—*homo homini lupus* (man is wolf to man)—came to the fore.

There may be those to say that my reading was less affected by the rise of neo-fascism and of the pro-slavery faction in the United States than it was by the heart-rending news from Aleppo and from Syria more generally. Fair enough. Pick your poison. And have our circumstances changed less than our focus, what we are now able to see? It may well be that there are some vital aspects of human existence and interdependence that we are coming to see more clearly, but this at the cost of losing sight of any number of other, more diverting phenomena.

> Alles Ständische und Stehende verdampft, alles Heilige wird entweiht, und die Menschen sind endlich gezwungen, ihre Lebensstellung, ihre gegenseitigen Beziehungen mit nüchternen Augen anzusehen. (*Manifest der Kommunistischen Partei*—The Communist Manifesto: All that is solid melts into air, all that is holy is profaned, and man is at last compelled to face with sober senses, his real conditions of life, and his relations with his kind.)

THE PROVERB *homo homini lupus* has been traced back through Freud and Hobbes to Plautus (c. 200 BC). In *Regarding the Pain of Others*, the specific idea, of our wolfishness, is implicit; Sontag states rather that, contrary to modern expectations and "modern ethical feeling, . . . War has been the norm and peace the exception." (She is speaking of military conflict; were we to focus instead on class warfare, we could find moments of greater and lesser murderousness, but there is no peace.)

Freud, writing around 1930, as the first tidal wave of fascism began to appear, was more explicit:

> [M]en are not gentle creatures, who want to be loved, who at the most can defend themselves if they are attacked; they are, on the contrary, creatures among whose instinctual endowments is to be reckoned a powerful share of aggressiveness. As a result, their neighbor is for them not only a potential helper or sexual object, but also someone who tempts them to satisfy their aggressiveness on him, to exploit his capacity for work without compensation, to use him sexually without his consent, to seize his possessions, to humiliate him, to cause him pain, to torture and to kill him. *Homo homini lupus*. . . . In circumstances that are favorable to it, when the mental counter-forces which ordinarily inhibit it are out of action, it also manifests itself spontaneously and reveals man as a savage beast to whom consideration towards his own kind is something alien.

I must point out that when we speak of "man," the category includes us, dear readers. It is more than a little unfortunate that *other* human beings are savage beasts, but the landscape explodes when we have the courage and clarity to accept that "I" am a savage beast, too. We didn't need Freud to remind us of this; the Greeks bequeathed us how many myths, plays, and histories of internecine warfare and of competition and murder within families? But of course such things stop none of us from deciding that "I" and my family, my group, and my country are exempt; we can only be some of the rare few who have suppressed or sublimated their savagery.

To this contention or decision, one could respond, Yeah, right, you're the enlightened, gentle ones—until it's a question of who is going to get the promotion, the sale, the helpful review, the larger share of the divorce settlement, the better preschool for her or his child, another country's oil or manual labor at bargain basement prices. But such a response misses the greater aggressiveness in which we are, however ignorantly, involved. Sontag touches on this when she makes this suggestion: "set aside the sympathy we extend to others beset by war and murderous politics for a reflection on how our privileges are located on the same map as their suffering, and may—in ways we might prefer not to imagine—be linked to their suffering as the wealth of some may imply the destitution of others."

To put this another way, the complexity and alienation of modern life obscures from the relatively well off—and allows us to ignore—how many of the comforts we enjoy are the (bitter?) fruits of brutal aggressiveness, not only of our ancestors, but also of corporations, government forces, and individuals active today. We might say that these groups and individuals have volunteered to do the killing and exploiting for us. And thus even as we enjoy our "privileges" (or our cheap oil, diamonds, coltan, water), we take pride in decrying the savagery of those—our mercenaries?—who are fighting the natural-resources-based wars in Syria, the Congo, Sudan, Mali . . . We would not have our sneakers or TVs be a whit more expensive, and we decry the working and living conditions of factory workers in the vast sweatshops of China and other, poorer countries.

Sontag notes that, although in the United States we have Holocaust museums, "there is no Museum of the History of Slavery—the whole story, starting with the slave trade in Africa itself, not just in selected parts, such as the Underground Railroad." Nor, I would add, is there a museum of the extermination of the American Indians, a sort of *Endlösung* (final solution) *avant la lettre,* and indeed a proceeding that inspired Hitler. Sontag writes:

> To have a museum chronicling the great crime that was African slavery in the United States of America would be to acknowledge that the evil was *here*. Americans prefer to picture the evil that was *there*, and from which the United States—a unique nation, one without any certifiably wicked leaders throughout its entire history—is exempt.

Some years ago, in *The Importance of Disappointment*, the English sociologist become psychologist Ian Craib sought to locate appropriate psychological and political responses to the stark reality of our savagery. Craib proposes:

> Psychological integration involves becoming aware of and putting up with authentically bad aspects of relationships with other people, *and* of one's self.

And,

> Given human nature and the limitation on our capacity to change, the political question becomes less "How do [we] make our society a better place to live?" and more "How do we prevent our society becoming a worse place?"

Augustine and his heirs and progenitors called (or made) the problem human corruption, original sin. Students of United States history can note how concerned James Madison and other framers of the Constitution were to make sure that it helped protect people from human weakness, viciousness certainly included. (Or did this supposed concern mask the real one: that in a democracy a wealthy minority risked being controlled by the more numerous poor and middle class? or by demagogues leveraging the power of these classes?) In any case, if we return to our epigraph and Sontag's point about the "perennially surprised that depravity exists" and about "moral or psychological adulthood," we might say that somewhere betwixt the late eighteenth century and November 8, 2016, many Americans—thanks to advertising? mass media? electronic devices?—had lost their maturity, lost their capacity to see others and themselves clearly. During this return to immaturity we once again saw through a glass, darkly. Now we are coming to face to face with the terms of our existence, gaining a capacity not only to know others, but also ourselves?

I WOULD APPEND to the present set of quotations and observations (savage in their own way?), a few comments that may seem to head in quite another direction, but thereby make important corollary and somewhat warmer points. The main one, which this piece will land on more than once, is that, despite human savagery, corruption, viciousness, whathaveyou, some human beings have enjoyed the luxury of serious reading and rumination. Let us not lose track of what wonderful luxuries these activities are.

Sontag proposes:

> There's nothing wrong with standing back and thinking. To paraphrase several sages: "Nobody can think and hit someone at the same time."

I cannot quite agree with the first of the two sentences. If standing back and thinking becomes a way of trying to avoid the fray—the incessant class warfare, among other things—or if standing back and thinking becomes a way of pretending to be above the fray, it is in bad faith and ultimately destructive. This because bad faith cannot lead to good—I mean insightful—thoughts and because, if intellectuals do not fight for their class interests, then their numbers and privileges will, sooner or later, decline.

In his semi-fictional revisting of the Spanish Civil War, *Soldados de Salamina* (2001), Javier Cercas has a character say "[A] mí me parece que un país civilizado es aquel en que uno no tiene necesidad de perder el tiempo con la política." (It seems to me that a civilized country is one in which one has no need to waste time on politics.) Sontag comes at this subject from another angle when she remarks that "nobody who really thinks about history can take politics altogether seriously." But Cercas and Sontag were writing in another time—a dozen years ago already—and our thoughts are ever responses to our circumstances. Post-Trump-election, I do not see how we can see politics as a waste of time or not take it altogether seriously. By this I do not mean *only* that defeating the fascists will, as during the Second World War, require massive mobilization. I also mean that it is hard now not to see—or recognize—what a vital, warm (though at times too warm) part of life politics is. It is part of being a human being, of being engaged with others, and it may offer some a cure for the loneliness and narcissism from which many now suffer. As Camus writes of Dr. Rieux, the hero of his *Plague*:

> Il avait seulement gagné d'avoir connu la peste et de s'en souvenir, d'avoir connu l'amitié et de s'en souvenir, de connaître la tendresse et de devoir un jour s'en souvenir. (A gloss: His only victory was to have known the plague and to be able to remember it, to

have known friendship and to remember it, to know tenderness and having one day to remember it, too.)

Perhaps even with Trump in the White House and the Koch Brothers pouring their oily money into the crusade to eliminate Social Security, I will yet live long enough to finally complete an essay on Camus's novel which I began many years ago. The heart of the graying draft remains this:

> One little noted difference between Doctor Rieux and his band and most of the other residents of the plague-infected city of Oran is that the first grouping are portrayed as having more fun. Through their commitment to fight for the survival of their community and of people they do not know, they find a rare companionship and a rare capacity for companionship. Striking, too, is how long their days are. After working like dogs dealing with the dead and dying and the government bureaucracy they still have time for long philosophical discussions, a dip in the sea. It is as if, because of their commitment, time for them is suspended or slowed down, their lives are larger than those of we ordinary mortals, focused as we are on our families, possessions, personal tastes, and private goals.

AND YET (AND FINALLY), all this championing of political engagement also highlights, by contrast, a point made implicitly by Sontag's writing and thinking, and by the book of it (*Regarding . . .*) that editors and designers helped her make. This point is, again: the opportunity and capacity to engage in serious reading and rumination are a great and wonderful luxury.

The contents of Sontag's book are so horrible—

> On the first day of the Battle of the Somme, July 1, 1916, sixty thousand British soldiers were killed or gravely wounded—thirty thousand of these in the first half-hour.
>
> American television viewers weren't allowed to see footage acquired by NBC (which the network then declined to run) of . . . the fate of thousands of Iraqi

> conscripts who, having fled Kuwait City at the end of the [Gulf War, 1991], were carpet bombed with explosives, napalm, radioactive DU (depleted uranium) rounds, and cluster bombs as they headed north . . . on the road to Basra, Iraq—a slaughter notoriously depicted by one American officer as a "turkey shoot."
>
> . . . the total extermination of the Herero people in Namibia decreed by the German colonial administration in 1904; the Japanese . . . massacre of nearly four hundred thousand, and the rape of eighty thousand, Chinese in December 1937 . . . ; the rape of some one hundred and thirty thousand women and girls (ten thousand of whom committed suicide) by victorious Soviet soldiers unleashed by their commanding officers in Berlin in 1945 . . .

And yet there is something so "civilized," if you will, something so pleasureful in Sontag's book, and notwithstanding how dispiriting and unpleasant its bits of history are. From whence does this civilization and pleasure spring? The slimness of the volume; a sense of breathing room offered by the ample leading between the lines of type and by the fact that there are only about 8 words per line, 200 per page. In part because she is Sontag, but mainly because she is of an older, pre-post-modern generation, Sontag also offers the comfort of absolute truths. She can tell us that 1945 was the year photographs' power "to define the most abominable realities trumped all the complex narratives" and that "photography is the only major art in which . . . " And my heart has a soft spot for lines such as the following, from *Regarding*'s Acknowledgments:

> For information about Roger Fenton [one of the first war photographers], I am indebted to Nathalie M. Houston, "Reading the Victorian Souvenir: Sonnets and Photographs of the Crimean War," *The Yale Journal of Criticism*, vol. 14, no. 2 (Fall 2001).
>
> I continue to learn, as I have for many years, from conversations with Ivan Nagel. [A Hungarian-German theater scholar and director.]

Much as, say, Plato's *Lysis*, these lines speak of a life of the mind, a life that currently seems in peril.

Notes

This is yet another essay that originally came with several thousand words of footnotes, words (and specific references) which may be found by searching out the version of this piece published on-line by *Zeteo* in December 2016. Below are three of the most salient notes.

[a] The "pro-slavery" compound has emerged, in my brain, as a result of a 2015 *New Yorker* piece currently much on my mind. The piece is Nicholas Lemann's *The Price of Union: The undefeatable South*, which suggests that not only has the Civil War never ended, the Southern side may be winning. A few extracts:

> A recent run of important historical studies have set themselves against the view of the antebellum South as a place apart, self-destructively devoted to its peculiar institution. Instead, they show, the South was essential to the development of global capitalism, and the rest of the country (along with much of the world) was deeply implicated in Southern slavery. Slavery was what made the United States an economic power. It also served as a malign innovation lab for influential new techniques in finance, management, and technology.

> [T]he passage of the Voting Rights Act was actually a North-South partnership, not an imposition of the North's will on the South. And it would be a big mistake to think of the act as a great, enduring civil-rights milestone, representing the country's belated decision to comply fully and everywhere with the Fifteenth Amendment to the Constitution. As Berman demonstrates, the act has been, instead, the subject of half a century of ceaseless contention, leaving its meaning permanently undetermined.

In the concluding paragraph, Lemann quotes from Lincoln's 1858 "House Divided" speech: "It will become all one thing or all the other." Perhaps we have yet to really find out which one it (we, the United States of America) will become.

[b] As regards the decimation of the American Indians and Adolf Hitler, one might see John Toland, *Adolf Hitler*:

> Hitler's concept of concentration camps as well as the practicality of genocide owed much, so he claimed, to his studies of English and United States history. He admired the camps for Boer prisoners in South Africa and for the Indians in the Wild West; and often praised to his inner circle the efficiency of America's extermination—by starvation and uneven combat—of the red savages who could not be tamed by captivity.

Writing in the *Jewish Journal* (on-line), Lia Mandelbaum goes further:

> [Hitler] was very interested in the way the Indian population had rapidly declined due to epidemics and starvation when the United States government forced them to live on the reservations. He thought the American government's forced migrations of the Indians over great distances to barren reservation land was a deliberate policy of extermination. Just how much Hitler took from the American example of the destruction of the Indian nations is hard to say; however, frightening parallels can be drawn. For some time Hitler considered deporting the Jews to a large 'reservation' in the Lubin area where their numbers would be reduced through starvation and disease.

[c] To explicate Sontag's "nobody who really thinks about history can take politics altogether seriously," I would begin in a Marxist, economic-determinist vein. For example, Middle Eastern politics, about which so much is made, can be seen as a dance choreographed by the value currently placed on oil. Should that value change significantly, the political dance will follow along. Similarly, in "What Does Socialism Mean Today?", reflections on the collapse of the Soviet Union, Jürgen Habermas wrote:

> It is not as though the collapse of the Berlin Wall [i.e. a

dramatic *political* event] has solved a single one of the problems specific to our system. The indifference of a market economy to its external costs, which it off-loads on to the social and natural environment, is sowing the path of a crisis-prone economic growth with the familiar disparities and marginalizations on the inside; with economic backwardness, if not regression, and consequently with barbaric living conditions, cultural expropriation, and catastrophic famines in the Third World; not to mention the worldwide risk caused by disrupting the balance of nature.

And then, thirdly, one could cite yet more fundamental forces, such as genetic ones. I have, for example, read that approximately 7,500 years ago, in a part of what is now Hungary, a genetic mutation occurred, allowing some number of humans to continue to be able to digest milk after the age of 8 or so. It has been proposed that the selective advantage of this single change may have helped the beneficiaries to take over Europe and establish a new way of life. In this case, the politics these people engaged in pales in significance when compared to their genetic endowment. (For more, see "The Milk Revolution: When a single genetic mutation first let ancient Europeans drink milk, it set the stage for a continental upheaval," by Andrew Curry, *Nature*.)

[23]
Almost Pure Pleasures

AT THE END OF A NATURE-PRESERVE COVE, I saw in the water some dark, complex something. Two box-like shapes, attached to one another. An abandoned part of a car engine? Approaching a little closer, I saw that it was two midsized, black-backed turtles, one clamped on the back of the other. They were rolling in the shallow water, and a stubby leg of the one on the bottom at times waved helplessly, and the one on top seemed at times to be nibbling at the neck of the partner-adversary underneath.

My assumption was that these turtles were having sex. Yet there were times—standing watching until nightfall—there were times I thought they were fighting—to the death? or like siblings?—or that the one on the bottom was being punished. Not being an amphibian, I could not help feeling that the turtle underneath, whose head was most always under water, was being drowned. A crime to which only I was witness, there not being another human anywhere nearby, and the birds in the tall grasses across the water happily chattering with one another.

In the movies the camera may do as I have just done: pull back to give viewers an idea of the larger scene, and also disengaging our minds from the action, leaving us freer to reflect on it. In writing, the "camera" (that is, the writer) can pull back yet further, giving readers the writer's own reflections. This strikes me now as a mixed blessing, as what I have to say is both basic and futile. Even a great nature filmmaker could not help. You had to be there, at the end of that cove—in the rapidly cooling, spring evening air, and lost to the sounds of cars, planes, human conversations—in order to feel—to feel viscerally—the terror, struggle, hard work, self-absorption, punishing and punishment, and pleasure and love of sex.

Among the information I took in later, Googling, was that a male turtle often stays clamped on the female's back and in her cloaca for quite some time (up to 24 hours)—trying to prevent other males from inseminating her. This effort, however prolonged, is rather futile, as the females, at least of some species, are able to store sperm for three years or more. They may well gather sperm from several males, and their eggs may end up fertilized by a range of males. In "compensation"—can it be called?—a male, in gripping tightly with his claws to the back of the female, often cuts into the soft flesh near her shell.

AFTERWARDS, WALKING AWAY, the pedestrian thought occurred to me that human sex lives must have been very different in centuries past when we grew up, not going to sex-education classes, but seeing around us other animals having sex. Under our sheets (or in our hay lofts), we must have been more in touch with what a primal act we animals were engaging in. For models—instead of those offered by the movies and porn sites—young people would have had turtles, pigs, horses, etc. And while a well-made "clip" might speak more directly to my twenty-first-century needs and desires, and thus, in a sense, be more inspiring, yet I found the fucking of these two turtles more erotic, indeed the most erotic event that I had ever seen. By way of explication I can only recall again the bottom turtle's fluttering leg, and my senses, or projections, of punishment and hard work, and a sense of these two beings locked together, and lost to the whole wide world, near and far. Temporarily they were living only for one another and for this task that they could not help but carry out to the best of their abilities and with what seemed to be the last of their strength.

Afterword—Social Comments

I watched these turtles in a preserve of several hundred acres where I, touring the whole of it in the course of several hours, encountered only three other people. I came to this preserve by riding on a bicycle two or three miles from a small town and along a neatly paved bike trail on which, going and returning, I encountered not one other bike rider. And on these same trails I had on other days ridden somewhat further to beaches which were deserted of humans because it was not "beach weather," though from the shore I could watch seals swimming.

While cycling, I passed many large, and yet more expensive, summer and weekend homes. It being a "shoulder season," the shades were drawn; the only sign of life an SUV or jeep, sitting not even stoically on the gravel driveway; the motor vehicle waiting to be rediscovered by its owners, currently driving other expensive cars in other expensive places.

I often recall how after the revolution, in the 1960s Hollywood movie *Doctor Zhivago*, the apartments of the Russian leisure class were turned into communal housing for the working classes. My home town, Manhattan, now has an increasing number of apartments that the global wealthy buy, not to live in, but to launder their money or try to preserve it against taxes and inflation.

After the next, American revolution, no one need sleep in shelters or on the street. Plenty of free space awaits and in "nice neighborhoods," which the revolution could empty of any not-at-all-nice people who proved slow in packing up their jewels and art works before fleeing to Mars or New Zealand.

While waiting, I have heard of celebrities who, with help from private jets, have been able, in a single day, to see and be seen at more than one famous, major-television-network event, in different parts of the world. The pleasure of such private-jetting or of knowing that somewhere, perhaps in several places, you have a very large house with the shades drawn and expensive cars in the driveway—let's call these "almost pure pleasures." The impurity comes from the fact that the pleasure depends on other, not-so-rich people—on there being many other people who do not have the money to do what you are doing or to have what you have.

And, cycling the deserted bike paths, and being passed by cars whose massiveness seemed needed above all for this—as a testament to the fact that "I" could own such a massive thing—along with "almost," the words "at least" came into my head. "Perhaps I will indeed die like everyone else, and perhaps it will be a gruesome death, or—on the way to this death, perhaps decades before it comes—I will know loneliness, fear, and frustration. But at least I have this big car, this very big house, this private jet." At least I am not like some other people or like people in general. (If only this could also mean that, unlike people in general, "I" was immortal.)

At least a writer of intellectual essays can say the same thing! And at least the government could use the private-jetters' money, however rotten, to fertilize more nature preserves, and pay for better and more ambitious public schools and health care. And at least—if we indeed lived in a democratic country?—might the life and culture of the United States not be so dominated by human beings whose lives have been given over to the almost pure pleasure of accumulating more money than other people have accumulated? Should we pray, too, that, in some unexpected future, male turtles will know if they're making babies or not, or won't care? And (in compensation?) could female turtles come to find the babymaking, or love-making, more pleasureful because their males were less clingy (or claw-y)?

My pleasure and awe, watching the turtles, was linked to the fact that I was the only person who was seeing, or could see, this sight. But my feelings had much more to do with what an extraordinary (and primal) sight it was (at least for an urban-dwelling, compulsive reader and writer such as myself). That we are animals, that is as sure as ever, and we may be reminded of it daily—in how savagely we behave toward one another and toward other species and inorganic others. And we can also be reminded of our animality when we rub more affectionately up against one another, or when we—however desperately—make love.

☙

[VI]
Backmatter

It is also the case that, after the most wonderful or transgressive love-making, and often after the most extravagant or delicate meals as well, one may regret what one has done and not done. It seems one has gone too far or not far enough.

— "On Savoring"

Where have we been?

If you have made it this far you will have formed your own opinions about what this book is about. A reader of an intermediate draft found its theme in the "On Savoring" essay, with its urging that we learn to sense not only the tasty and orally pleasing, but also, say, the cost of rent or the exploitation of immigrant labor in a restaurant meal. Bad coffee may be savored for its badness and sad moments for their sadness, as much as the joyous for their more agreeable qualities. More broadly, the essays have proposed that a life engaged in fully tasting, sensing, appreciating the life one is indeed living may be fuller than one devoted to escape and denial.

On another plane, more pragmatically, this book has offered samples—highlights, I would like to call them—from a range of writing done these past few years, years preceding more than following the 2016 US presidential election. And yet that event now casts backward a long shadow, which cannot be ignored. As the beginning of "Collage, TV President, Bonnard, Miró" put it, in the aftermath of Trump's election, there came a feeling that all had changed, and that the work of writers and artists had also to change somehow. Ideally, our new approach would also be effective, re-righting the ship or grounding it on a more appealing shore (which we would also savor for its less-appealing qualities?).

Some readers will recall that recovering our dreams—my dreams—was a theme of the previous collection: *Surviving the Twenty-First Century*, and particularly of the essay "Where are our dreams?" (the first version of which is available on-line, at Montaigbakhtinian.com). Instead of here quoting myself, I will slip away to a short Vachel Lindsay poem from 1915, "The Leaden-Eyed":

> Let not young souls be smothered out before
> They do quaint deeds and fully flaunt their pride.
> It is the world's one crime its babes grow dull,
> Its poor are oxlike, limp and leaden-eyed.

> Not that they starve, but starve so dreamlessly;
> Not that they sow, but that they seldom reap;
> Not that they serve, but have no gods to serve;
> Not that they die, but that they die like sheep.

THE WORD "DIALOGUE" HAS OFTEN APPEARED IN THIS BOOK, starting certainly in the second essay, if not in the first. In that second piece, "Drawing, Conversation, Life," it was proposed that an ideal conversation is like a sea-blown boat. We might wonder if a reader come to such a collection of essays is more like the boat, the water, or the wind. Certainly it is the possibility of readers that gives texts their force and direction.

In the essay on Plato and "Friendship, Deception, Writing" it was proposed that the essence of friendship is rubbing and being rubbed by other human beings. That writers have developed a particular, *voire* peculiar, way of doing such rubbing may underscore their (our) desperation, along with our capacity for finding what Freud called *Ersatzbefriedigungen*: substitutive satisfactions. In any case, the dialogue between a book and a reader is a wonderful thing, if also sad or pristine because the rubbing is so ethereal.

Of course nowadays, and particularly in big cities such as New York, where I live, most of the rubbing is between strangers. And well suited to savoring for its badness? No, let's not say that! In "Guston, Schapiro, Rosenberg, . . . Dialogue" I recounted how once I asked a stranger in a New York art gallery why she thought the artist had made the paintings on display. We might say that her reply—"I'm not going to answer that. That's such a dumb question"—was a gift, at least to a writer, insofar as it was the impetus for a whole essay.

IT'S A FORM OF RISK TAKING—full of courage and idealism—to try to explore ideas and feelings with other people. Thus, dear readers, I welcome both your counter punches and your kisses and your ruminations, and even though I may strain to feel them across seas lying between us. If you could please first spell your first name and last name and clearly state the account number that appears on the back of your bill, the last four digits of your Social Security number, your zip code and your birthdate . . . No. This was just to note that with the Flag at Half-Mast, Carol, and Beauty of the System pieces, I have sought to leave room for satire.

WHEN THE TITLE *ART, SEX, POLITICS* APPEARED IN MY MIND, it seemed natural, sexy, and accurate. The essays collected in this volume are about art, sex, and politics, and often about more than one of these subjects at once. I later realized, however, that the combination of these things—of art and sex and politics—provides more than just a label; it speaks to a fundamental feature of the American experience. At an extreme there are groups like the Shakers whose wondrous music and dancing and austere "politics" (in the sense both of doctrines and of community) were founded on sexual repression. Or, as the scholar John McKelvie Whitworth has put it: many of the younger members of the Shaker sect

> appear to have sublimated their sexual energies, and possibly their procreative desires, in the only way open to them—by developing high standards of craftsmanship and expending considerable energy and effort to improve the practical arrangements of the "earthly heavens."

Quite otherwise, and yet retaining this fundamental connection of art, sex, and politics, in the post-World-War-II period secular champions of progressive politics (and of new products) have also been proponents and practitioners of traditionally taboo sexual practices and supporters of non-traditional approaches to art (far from Shaker simplicity and craftsmanship). If I may be allowed an offhand remark: we used to have "blue movies"; now we have blue states.

But may such theorizing and wise-cracking not obscure the fact that in this collection I have been pleased to be able in a few places to speak more directly about animality and about human animal desires. I will here allow myself to reprise some earlier lines.

- From "Professional Primates": A Freudian might speak of sublimation, of how some of us rise above our animal instincts. This would be to ignore how often such "sublimation" is not so much a rising above as a pretending to be other than we really are.
- From the "Sonnet for 9/27": Breastfeeding may soon be all that is left.
- From "Dickinson's Dying Tiger": Even if something like water has, finally, been found, and even if the speaker is preparing for the beast to lick the wetness—it's too late. The animal has died.
- From the last lines of the last essay, "Almost Pure Pleasures": That we are animals, that is as sure as ever, and we may be reminded of it daily—how savagely we behave toward one another and toward other species and inorganic others. And we can also be reminded of our animality when we rub more affectionately up against one another, or when we—however desperately—make love.

Amen.

Thanks!

Allow me to thank several people who played central roles in the development of this collection. For the past half dozen years I have been the Editor of *Zeteo*, an (or the) on-line journal for readers and thinkers. Many of the pieces in *Art, Sex, Politics* first appeared in *Zeteo*. I thank all *Zeteo* colleagues—and particularly Diana Bahr, Cat Gironda, Theona Kastens, Gayle Rodda Kurtz, Ed Mooney, Alexia Raynal, and Steve Webb—for their excellent editorial suggestions and intellectual companionship. I also thank the staff at *Agni*—particularly the editors Sven Birkerts, William Pierce, and Jennifer Alise Drew—for their contributions to my work, of which the Plato essay is but one example. Recently Noël Fost, working from Luxembourg, and I have collaborated on French versions of my essays, stories, and poems that begin their public lives at Montaigbahktinian.com. It has been a great pleasure working with Noël, and his ideas have not only improved the French texts, but also led to improvements in the English. Molly Renda most generously and brilliantly provided the cover design. Walter Cummins, who has been the ruthless (hardly!) tsar of Serving House Books, not only pressed me to put together this follow-up to our previous *Surviving the Twenty-First Century*, he has been a guiding light in shaping the contents and indeed was an early reader and editor of many of the pieces.

Above all, I thank my son Jonah, who—now getting ready to go off to college and get on with his life—has long been my steady companion, daily fielding my ideas and offering me his own. Further, and beyond the call of duty for a teenager, night after night when I came home from my drawing sessions he photographed the results. His mother once said that there was nothing worse than having to read your father's love poems. Second prize: having to photograph Papa's rude attempts to draw naked people or fruit?

READERS, DON'T BE SHY. Please feel free to e-mail any comments or reflections to me at Eaton0824@gmail.com. Writing and drawing are quite self-involved activities, but they are also one of the strange ways humans have come up with for reaching out toward other humans. Reaching out—and, at times, touching—is our most significant artistic, sexual, and political act.

Ways of Skipping Around
A few notes for extra-curious readers

In general readers will find that each of the five sections is a mix of shorter pieces which lead up to or tiptoe away from one longer piece. They may also note that—section headings be damned—many of the pieces in each section touch on more than one of the basic topics: art, sex, and politics. And there are themes and favorite authors and texts that reappear. Below is a list of some of these and of roughly where they may be found.

2016 United States presidential election: *DON'T HATE ME HATE; Guston Presidents Cartoons Questions?; Collage, TV President, Bonnard, Miró; Sontag, Hell, Thinking, Politics*

The American Indians: *Collage, TV President, Bonnard, Miró; Ditch the Term Pathogen; Sontag, Hell, Thinking, Politics*

Animals or animality: *On Savoring; Dickinson's Dying Tiger; On Shunga and Learning How to Feel What When; Professional Primates; The Beauty of the System; Almost Pure Pleasures*

John Cage: *On Savoring; Guston, Schapiro, Rosenberg, . . . Dialogue*

Capitalism: *On Savoring; Dickinson's Dying Tiger; Guston, Schapiro, Rosenberg, . . . Dialogue; Professional Primates; Ditch the Term Pathogen; Bologna Postmodernism Bob Perelman Amis; Sontag, Hell, Thinking, Politics*

Ian Craib: *On Savoring; Sontag, Hell, Thinking, Politics*

Cyrano de Bergerac: *Guston Presidents Cartoons Questions?; Friendship, Deception, Writing*

Exploration: *Distancing/Awareness, In Kant's Wood, Friendship, Deception, Writing*

Fellow Feeling: *The Third Man; The Beauty of the System*

Freud: *The Third Man; Dickinson's Dying Tiger; Professional*

Primates; Ditch the Term Pathogen; Friendship, Deception, Writing; Sontag, Hell, Thinking, Politics

"From such crooked wood as man is made, nothing perfectly straight can be built": *In Kant's Wood; Friendship, Deception and Writing*

Homo homini lupus (man is wolf to man) & the "*ungesellige Gesellgkeit des Menschen*" (the unsocial sociability of human beings): *In Kant's Wood, Sontag, Hell, Thinking, Politics*

The Jungle: *Professional Primates; The Third Man*

The Lorax (Dr. Seuss): *In Kant's Wood; Professional Primates*

James Madison: *In Kant's Wood; Sontag, Hell, Thinking, Politics*

Manhattan apartments: *On Savoring; Collage, TV President, Bonnard, Miró; Professional Primates; NRALGBTQ; Almost Pure Pleasures*

Marx: *On Savoring; Guston, Schapiro, Rosenberg, . . . Dialogue; In Kant's Wood; Sontag, Hell, Thinking, Politics*

Modern choreography: *Dickinson's Dying Tiger; Collage, TV President, Bonnard, Miró; Sontag, Hell, Thinking, Politics*

The Movies: *The Third Man; Carol, Rooney! Smoking? Gun; Distancing/Awareness; Collage, TV President, Bonnard, Miró; Almost Pure Pleasures*

Nietzsche: *Guston, Schapiro, Rosenberg, . . . Dialogue; Distancing/Awareness; Ditch the Term Pathogen*

Opportunism: *The Third Man; Bologna Postmodernism Bob Perelman Amis; Sontag, Hell, Thinking, Politics*

Paris: *DON'T HATE ME, HATE; On Savoring*

Adam Philllips: *On Savoring; In Kant's Wood*

Plato's *Lysis*: *Guston, Schapiro, Rosenberg, . . . Dialogue; Friendship, Deception and Writing; Sontag, Hell, Thinking, Politics*

Product placement: *Carol, Rooney! Smoking? Gun; Collage, TV President, Bonnard, Miró*

Quakerism: *Guston Presidents Cartoons Questions?*; *Bologna Postmodernism Bob Perelman Amis*

Satire: *Carol, Rooney! Smoking? Gun*; *The American Flag is at Half-Mast Today*

Sociology of science: *Guston, Schapiro, Rosenberg, . . . Dialogue; Distancing/Awareness; Professional Primates; Ditch the Term Pathogen; The Beauty of the System*

Socrates: *My Evening with Marta; On Savoring; The Third Man; Guston, Schapiro, Rosenberg, . . . Dialogue; Ditch the Term Pathogen; Friendship, Deception and Writing*

Essays that do not find themselves cited above, and thus may claim to be more *sui generis*, more autonomous?

Drawing, Conversation, Life

Sonnet for 9/27

About the Author

In between drawings, William Eaton has been an award-winning journalist, novelist, writer of erotic fiction, intellectual essays, and dialogues. *Surviving the Twenty-First Century*, a collection of his essays from Montaigbakhtinian.com, was published by Serving House in 2015. One of Eaton's dialogues, *The Professor of Ignorance Condemns the Airplane*, was staged in New York in 2014. He is the Editor of *Zeteo: The Journal of Interdisciplinary Writing*. He holds graduate degrees from Columbia and the City University of New York, and a B.A. from the University of California at Berkeley.

Made in the USA
Columbia, SC
13 January 2018